Forty Years a Forester

ANNOTATED EDITION

ELERS KOCH

Edited and with an
introduction by Char Miller
Foreword by John N. Maclean

University of Nebraska Press
LINCOLN

Library of Congress Cataloging-in-Publication Data
Names: Koch, Elers, 1880–1954, author. |
Miller, Char, 1951– editor.
Title: Forty years a forester / Elers Koch;
edited and with an introduction by Char
Miller; foreword by John N. Maclean.
Description: Annotated edition. | Lincoln: University
of Nebraska Press, [2019] | "Chapter 12 first appeared
in Journal of Forestry 33, no. 2, 98–104. Reprinted
by permission of the Society of American Foresters."
Includes bibliographical references and index.
Identifiers: LCCN 2019005316
ISBN 9781496213358 (paperback: alk. paper)
ISBN 9781496217240 (epub)
ISBN 9781496217257 (mobi)
ISBN 9781496217264 (pdf)
Subjects: LCSH: Koch, Elers, 1880–1954. |
Foresters—Montana—Biography. | United States.
Forest Service—Officials and employees—Biography.
Classification: LCC SD129.K63 A3 2019 |
DDC 634.9092 [B]—dc23 LC record available
at https://lccn.loc.gov/2019005316

Set in Garamond Premier by E. Cuddy.
Designed by N. Putens.

To the men and women of the Forest Service—
past and present

CONTENTS

ILLUSTRATIONS

FOREWORD

John N. Maclean

Back in the 1950s, the arrival of a living legend created no small stir here in our remote corner of northwestern Montana. Elers Koch, whose family owned the lakeside cabin next to ours, had been a leader in the landmark battle against the great fires of 1910, when the woods roared in the panhandle of Idaho and our part of Montana, firestorms that drove forest management for generations. A native Montanan, Koch had graduated from the Yale School of Forestry to become one of Pinchot's Young Men, the first rangers of the U.S. Forest Service under its first chief, Gifford Pinchot. Koch had gone on to a distinguished regional post within the agency, which in those days ran the nation's public woodlands with virtually undisputed authority, before his eventual retirement.

Koch was a man of slight physical build but remarkable physical abilities, a fine horseman and extraordinary hiker, said to knock off ten miles after dinner to make an even twenty for the day. But he was also a thinker and writer. He bravely published an article a quarter of a century after the fires of 1910, advocating a let-burn policy for wildfire, at a time when Forest Service higher-ups favored—and then institutionalized—a policy of full suppression of all fires. Observing the result of the vast efforts to control fire, he had asked a question that reverberates to this day, "Has all this effort and expenditure of millions of dollars added anything to human good? Is it possible that it was all a ghastly mistake like plowing up the good buffalo grass sod of the dry prairies?"

When we heard the news of his pending visit, the event took on the aura of a historic occasion, although to Koch himself it was a pilgrimage of old age to his cabin on Seeley Lake, a place he had loved long and well.

In many ways, the Koch family and mine had grown up together with the Forest Service. Our two families had built summer cabins on the lake next to each other in the 1920s with no electricity, no heat except a fireplace, and no indoor plumbing but for a water line from the lake to a faucet in the kitchen. Our cabin sites, leased from the Forest Service, lay beneath an extraordinary stand of western larch trees that had been saved from the logger's axe. Koch, who had studied them, described the stand as "unique and as beautiful in its way as the better known redwoods." In an article for *American Forests* magazine in 1945, he reported counting 915 growth rings on one fallen giant, making it nearly a millennium old. Pinchot, who had backpacked the Swan Valley just to the north of us in 1896, also loved the larch and called them his "favorite American tree."

Who or what act of man had saved our larch stand had always remained something of a mystery, at least until recent years. Ron Cox, a retired forester and mainstay of the Seeley Lake Historical Society, has researched the matter and determined it was no single person and no single act. He credits Ambrose Norton, Forest Service Lumberman (an actual title of the day), for beginning the process of preserving our larch when he was in charge of a massive timber sale in 1906 on the east side of Seeley Lake, opposite from our cabins. Norton, with a romantic flair, ordered the preservation of a "belt of trees" along what is now Highway 83 to preserve the "wildness and beauty . . . whispering its story to the winds of the Rockies." Norton's "belt of trees" landed him in trouble with superiors, just as the let-burn article later did with Koch, and for this and other reasons he was transferred to Wyoming. His successor in charge of the timber sale was Jim Girard, a timber cruiser whose original method of scaling logs remains in use today. In a letter to Pinchot, Girard described Norton, the man he replaced, as a "gentleman and scholar" who was "intensely concerned with the interests of the Forest Service, but was unfamiliar with western conditions [or] the lumberman's problems." Norton's many proposals to protect trees, Girard wrote to Pinchot, would have "broken any company with limited resources." Cox speculates, however, that Forest Service personnel, impressed by Norton's set-aside, saw the wisdom of preserving the larch on our side of

FIG. 1. (*top*) Elers and Gerda Koch at Seeley Lake. (*bottom*) The Koch family at their cabin on Seeley Lake (next door to the Maclean family cabin), circa 1940. Photos by Stanley H. Koch.

the lake, a recreational magnet that soon included cabin leases, a game preserve, and a planned chalet or hotel that never materialized. Today, the 60-acre grove of larch near our cabin, including one giant about one thousand years old, rated the largest in North America, is dedicated to Girard, who after his start at Seeley Lake went on to become a Forest Service legend himself.

Koch's visit had special significance for my father, Norman, who had worked for the Forest Service as a teenager and had long revered Elers Koch. Both men had headed east to pursue higher education, but unlike Koch, my father had decided against a Forest Service career and instead had chosen a starkly different path as a professor of English at the University of Chicago. Eventually my father would find a way to bring his two worlds—Montana and the life of the mind—together. But his yearning for the kind of life Koch had lived so successfully in the mountains and forests of the Northern Rockies gnawed at him with animal intensity. He was now spending hours at a time prepping my mother, Jessie, my sister, Jean, and me on the importance of the coming visit, both as an event in itself and as a chance to ask questions about the men, policies, and forests Koch had known.

When the great day arrived, we were asked to stay away until evening to give Koch time to rest and be with his family. At the appointed hour, my father led us along the path through huckleberry bushes and kinni-kinnick, under the towering larch trees, for the gathering at the Koch cabin. Koch, who in his younger days had ridden horseback sixty miles each summer from Missoula to Seeley Lake and then back, was helped out onto the cabin porch, now in evening shadow, and settled into a chair. We gathered round, the young like me finding spots on the floor at his feet. In the dim light we looked up at a small man of great age with a pair of startlingly large eyes set deeply into the nearly translucent skin drawn tight across his face. He said something in a muffled voice, and hovering women scurried to take down an old, dusty buffalo robe from the wall and wrap it around him. With his body enveloped by the robe, the eyes seemed to become more prominent, and they scanned us like beams from a lighthouse.

We settled down and my father took out his notebook with its questions. I do not remember what he asked, but Koch responded with long silences and very few words. My father grew frustrated, speaking more loudly, more insistently. Eventually those large prominent eyes dimmed and shifted downward, and something muffled was said: the brief interview came to an end, leaving my father feeling empty. The Koch aura has stuck with me, however, as an image of a tribal elder with a mystical and powerful connection to the land we all loved: Seeley Lake and its larch.

Koch did not live to see the vindication of his brave stance in favor of healthy fire. As our family walked the path back to our cabin that night, we did not understand how the larch towering over our heads had grown so massive—we figured at the time it was an *absence* of fire. After years of research, however, Forest Service scientists determined that frequent low-intensity fires were a healthy thing to be encouraged, and that such fires, ignited by Native Americans and lightning in the years before the full suppression policy, had regularly cleared undergrowth and allowed the larch of Seeley Lake to become giants. In more recent years, when the Seeley Lake ranger, Tim Love, oversaw a thinning and burning project near the lake to mimic the effects of good natural fire, it was met with opposition, and it took courage and persistence to get the job done. Koch would have felt a bond of kinship with Ranger Love.

That thinning project, though, involved only a few thousand acres. Three major wildland fires have burned close to Seeley Lake in the years since, after nearly a century of no major fires. That's partly a consequence of the full suppression policy, but other significant factors—logging, absence of logging, beetle kill, and climate change among them—have had their effect as well. Ours is a complex, evolving ecosystem with great challenges ahead. Koch's legacy—of close observation of the natural world, original thought, and the courage to express a conviction—helps answer the question my father might have asked him that evening on the cabin porch long ago: how do we proceed from here?

FIG. 2. Elers Koch at ease in his rose garden, probably in 1952.

FORTY YEARS A FORESTER

INTRODUCTION

Char Miller

"It is well to go all out sometimes."
—ELERS KOCH

It is not every day that a real-life American forester becomes a character in a novel.[1] Gifford Pinchot, founding chief of the U.S. Forest Service, may have inaugurated this sub-sub-genre in American literature when he appeared by name in Hamlin Garland's *Cavanagh, Forest Ranger: A Romance of the Mountain West* (1910); to this potboiler he also contributed the foreword.[2] Odd though Pinchot's crossover act may have been, one of his most valued forest rangers, Elers Koch, managed to upstage his boss. Not only did Koch's illustrious four-decade career in the Forest Service receive considerable praise in Ivan Doig's *English Creek* (1984), but the Montana-born-and-based forester tried his hand at fiction; Koch set his only novel, *The High Trail* (1953), within the rugged mountains of his native state and neighboring Idaho. However stiff its characters, the landscapes that Koch sketches and through which his characters move are vividly rendered, a result of Koch having spent a lifetime hiking through nearly every valley, trekking through many of the region's foothills, and ascending many of its tallest, granite-faced peaks. Along the way, forester Koch had surveyed this vast domain, camped

FIG. 3. Elers Koch reading, undated.

and fished along its ice-cold rushing rivers, and had chased after (and raced from) furious wildland fires.[3]

Koch's larger-than-life presence was what so captivated novelist Doig, who also grew up in the Treasure State. He made ready use of Koch's experiences in *English Creek*, one of a trilogy of novels about the transformation of what the novelist called Two Medicine country, a fictionalized terrain set in the northern Rockies. The eponymous national forest, and the forest rangers who stewarded its broad expanse, set *English Creek*'s physical context and some of its very human challenges. To help readers understand how these invaluable public lands came into being in the first place, and the enormity of the effort and energy that went into their creation in the early twentieth century, Doig introduced Koch through the voice of Jick McCaskill, son of a second-generation forester on the Two Medicine National Forest: "In any Forest Service family such as ours, lore of setting up national forests, of the boundary examiners who established them on the maps of America as public preserves was almost holy writ. I could remember time upon time hearing my father and other Forest Service men of his age mention those original rangers and supervisors, the ones sent out in the first years of the century with not much more than a legal description of a million or so acres and orders to transform them in a national forest." These men's transformative impact earned them the nickname "forest arrangers." Elers Koch was among those around whom "tales . . . still circulated," Jick McCaskill recalled from the vantage point of the punishing Great Depression, and who were "refreshed by the comments of younger rangers wondering how they'd managed to do all they had. Famous, famous guys. Sort of combinations of Old Testament prophets and mountain men, rolled up into one."[4]

Koch might have laughed at Jick and Doig's encomium. He might have winced at the similarly heroic vision embedded in the frontispiece photograph, "The Ranger," that adorned Garland's earlier novel. Set between two pines, a forester and his valued horse—their backs to the viewer—stare west across a retreating series of mountain ranges, an immense domain to which man and beast seemed to announce and embody a civilizing force. As one of Garland's characters observes: "Each year sees the Old West diminish, and already, in the work of the Forest Service, law and order advance."[5] Koch might have felt conflicted about such praise—direct or indirect—but in truth his legendary career in the Forest Service, and the formative influence that it had on the ground, was in line with what these very different novelists imagined; in their hands, fiction and fact converged.

Nothing makes this case quite as forcefully as Koch's memoir and *its* frontispiece image. Astride his favorite horse and outfitted in full Forest Service uniform, from boot to hat, the confident rider faces forward and at an oblique angle, not quite catching the viewer's eye. This statuesque pose reinforces the forester's stature: he is a man on a mission, a framing that evokes the way in which his individual aspirations fused with institutional objectives. "I think I was born to be a forester," Koch professes in the first sentence of his memoir, and the timing of his coming-of-age could not have been more propitious, because "the profession of forestry in the United States opened up just in time to offer me the kind of life and work that fit my desires and upbringing."[6] By joining his biography with the agency's history, by splicing together the personal and professional, Koch asserts one of the central themes of *Forty Years a Forester*.

Family first. Born in December 1880, the oldest son of Peter and Laurentze Koch, Elers grew up in a household rife with stories of migration and pioneering. His father had emigrated from Denmark to the United States in the mid-1860s. Seeking his fortune, Peter Koch found hardship instead, and like many other migrants, moved from state to state in search of work. A sense of a stable future and beckoning opportunity came conjoined when he arrived at his seafaring uncle's home in southern Mississippi; among the twelve cousins that Peter met at his relative's sprawling farmstead, one of them, Laurentze, caught his eye. He was equally attracted to the prospect of a gold strike then reported in the upper Missouri watershed. Whether the young couple pledged their troth before Peter worked for his passage on a steamboat heading up the Mississippi River is unknown. Whatever vows they made then, they kept their promise, marrying nearly a decade later in 1874.

The couple timed their nuptials to Peter's emerging entrepreneurial success. After knocking around the Missouri headwaters without much success—Koch wryly noted on his twenty-fifth birthday that he was "still poor as a church rat"—he made his way to the relatively new settlement of Bozeman, Montana, and there began to make his mark. By the early 1870s he had demonstrated a talent for leadership and logistics, as well as accounting and surveying, all skills local merchants and ranchers prized. In time, his expansive commercial interests and scientific avocations enabled him to contribute significantly to the establishment and administration of Montana State College (now University) in Bozeman.[7]

Home to an estimated two thousand people when Elers Koch was born there, Bozeman was set within a vast, well-drained, and mountainous territory, the perfect backdrop for a vigorous life in the Great Outdoors. As Koch recounts, he, his parents, and his younger brother, Stanley, spent as much time as they could in nature, fishing the Gallatin

River, riding up into the Bridger and Gallatin ranges, camping, hiking, and recreating. Education was as important as exercise. Elers's father, a self-trained naturalist and a compelling teacher, was eager to pass along what he had absorbed and observed to his progeny. "To this day the greater number of Latin names I carry in my mind for plants are the ones I learned from my father," Elers observed. "It is just as easy for a boy that a plant is called *mertensia* or *Douglassi* as to call it blue bell or pink moss."[8] Scientists, surveyors, and historians visiting Bozeman found their way to the Koch family's dinner table, adding to the boy's wealth of knowledge. It is hard to imagine a set of environments and experiences more conducive to a career in forestry than those Elers Koch encountered on foot and horseback, or while warming his hands over a pine-scented campfire or the family hearth.

As if a link between his passion and profession was preordained, and like Koch himself, forestry as an idea and social institution came of age in the late nineteenth century. The 1870s were especially pivotal to the development of the emerging conception that Americans might more sustainably live on and within the land. Among the seminal texts that helped redefine this conception of the human place in the natural world—and why Americans needed to think more carefully about how they utilized natural resources—was George Perkins Marsh's *Man and Nature; or, Physical Geography as Modified by Human Action* (1864). This lengthy tome shrewdly analyzed the Industrial Revolution's devastating impact on the environment and offered its many readers an alternative approach; conservative stewardship, Marsh argued, would protect the Earth from human excess. To jolt his fellow citizens into action, Marsh warned of a coming apocalypse that would destroy the young nation if not restrained through a dramatic change in attitude and behavior. The founders of the American Forest Association, established in 1875, heeded his cautionary words. So did those who read widely in the emerging European literature on forestry and conservation that Marsh himself had depended on to make his case. Some of these reformers went further, corresponding with or studying under British, French, and German foresters to absorb European theories and practices of scientific forest management, assessing whether these concepts could be transferred across the Atlantic. At least some of these curious travelers published their reflections in *Garden & Forest* (1888–97), a New York–based periodical devoted to and a clearinghouse for the conservation cause.[9]

This intellectual engagement and political activism produced a small, if barely noticed, bureaucratic breakthrough—the 1876 creation of a Special Agent within the Department of Agriculture to monitor the health and extent of forests in the United States. Five years later, this single position morphed into the tiny Division of Forestry, and in 1891 Congress passed a key piece of legislation known as the Organic Act to create national forest reserves through presidential proclamation. Because this initial legislation said nothing about who would administer these reserves, or how they would do so, in 1897 Congress fixed this oversight by granting the Executive Branch the authority to regulate these new reserves. This so-called Management Act came with a set of managerial objectives: "No public forest reservation shall be established, except to improve and protect the forest within the reservation [boundaries], or for the purpose of securing favorable conditions of water flows, and to furnish a continuous supply of timber for the use and necessities of citizens of the United States."[10]

Left unaddressed was who the government would hire to guard and steward these designated public lands—from Colorado's White River Forest Reserve and Wyoming's Yellowstone Park Timberland Reserve, both designated in 1891, to California's San Gabriel Mountains Timberland Reserve, designated in 1892. The answer lay in the invention of a new occupation, a new social type: the forest ranger. To fill this employment opportunity, a clutch of academic institutions quickly established training programs at the undergraduate and graduate levels. The Biltmore Forest School and the New York State College of Forestry at Cornell University, both founded in 1898, set the stage for the establishment of the Yale Forest School in 1900; with a lead donation from Gifford Pinchot and his family, the Yale program offered the nation's first graduate degree in forestry. Shortly thereafter, the profession of forestry surged into being, with the launch of the Society of American

Foresters in 1900 and the publication of the *Journal of Forestry*. There was plenty of work available for the first cohort of forestry students. Between 1891 and 1905, Republican and Democratic presidents redesignated upwards of 85 million acres of the public domain as forest reserves. In 1905, Theodore Roosevelt, working in close coordination with Pinchot, the fourth head of the then-landless USDA Bureau of Forestry, signed a congressional act that transferred these forests and grasslands from the Department of the Interior to the Department of Agriculture. As part of the transfer, Congress agreed to the formation of a new agency, the U.S. Forest Service, to oversee these public lands and regulate the use of their natural resources.[11]

None of these alterations occurred in a vacuum; they depended on parallel changes in the nation-state itself. Indeed, rangers could not implement forestry principles on the ground without what German-born forester Bernhard Fernow, who was Pinchot's immediate predecessor in the Department of Agriculture's forestry office, had argued for in 1895— the creation of a paternal and perpetual government whose "providential functions" superseded local governance.[12] Ensuring this priority animated the conservation politics that President Roosevelt and Pinchot then pursued between 1900, when Roosevelt became president following William B. McKinley's assassination, and 1909, when Roosevelt left the White House. For nearly a decade, Pinchot hired Yale-trained foresters like Elers Koch to survey, assess, and patrol the lands under the agency's control, and fought and won in the courts for these managers' right to enforce user fees for grazing, mining, and lumbering. In sanctioning the agency's actions, the U.S. Supreme Court extended the federal government's sovereignty and legitimized a new approach to land management, which, in Pinchot words, was "the greatest good, for the greatest number in the long run."[13]

Although far from the centers of national debate and political power, Montana was every bit as connected to these transformations as the District of Columbia. Like many other western states, the creation of the first forest reserves in Montana often sparked controversy. The Flathead Reserve, for example, had been proposed in 1891 as a method to protect forests along the upper reaches of the Missouri and Columbia rivers, a proposal that met with stout resistance. The state's surveyor general spoke for many of its local opponents when he denounced the forest reserves scheme: "I regard such suggestions as emanating from the brain of a mad man." General Land Office surveyor A. E. Leach relayed this persistent pushback to his superiors in Washington, noting that he had "as yet to find a single man who is in sympathy with the scheme, and that every man with whom he conversed is bitterly opposed to any such reserve." That early plan was set aside, but the reaction was as noisy six years later when President Cleveland finally and formally established the Flathead. Mining and timber companies; livestock operators; and local, state, and congressional politicians sought to rescind the declaration; it was a bitter, albeit unsuccessful, campaign that complicated the forest's management for years to come.[14]

Yet many of these same public officials who fought assiduously against the reserves and the later establishment of the national forest system proved invaluable supporters of the University of Montana's ambition to establish a forestry school in Missoula—the purpose of which would be to train those who would regulate the same public lands these politicians routinely denounced. They cheered university president Charles Duniway's assertion that eastern elite institutions such as Cornell, Yale, and Harvard had little understanding of western resource issues and his conviction that the state university could do better. The time was also right, Duniway declared in his 1908 inaugural address:

> We miss a splendid opportunity of service to the state as long as we fail to give professional training to our young men who are being attracted into the new field of forestry, which has for its object the conservation of our natural resources. The choice of Missoula as one of the great districts of the National Forest Service gives us a direct contact with this work second to none in the United States.[15]

Elers Koch knew whereof Duniway spoke. His undergraduate experience at the state college in Bozeman, which he had entered in the fall of 1897 as a member of the class of 1901, testified to the need for a more robust curriculum in forestry, a need that the Missoula campus finally would fulfill in 1913. Still, even if forestry had been in the curriculum, it is not clear that Elers would have majored in it. Koch's father had encouraged his son to study broadly before specializing, and so Elers remembers taking what amounted to an intense liberal arts curriculum, including courses in the sciences and humanities as well as those in ancient and modern languages. Certain that his talented child's engagement with the natural world suggested he might have a knack for forestry, the senior Koch, a long-time university board member, also promoted a course of lectures on the subject by Lt. George P. Ahern, a self-taught forestry advocate. Elers did some fieldwork with Ahern, and it was through Ahern's contacts that in 1899 the young man secured what would prove a life-changing summer position as a student assistant in Gifford Pinchot's Bureau of Forestry, spending three months in Washington State.

"There were about twenty men in the crew," Koch later wrote, "most of them Harvard, Yale, or Princeton men," and while many were from "distinguished families . . . I got along fine with them in spite of the fact that I was almost the only western man in the party. They knew a lot of things I didn't, but I knew how to get around the woods better than they did." They'd also had one vital experience he had not: they had met the charismatic Gifford Pinchot, who convinced them to "try this new forestry thing." These neophyte foresters could not resist Pinchot's alluring message about the individual opportunities and social import of their future work. The "field is practically untouched," Pinchot told a group of Yale students in a speech he would deliver at one college after another. Its very newness meant that "a forester finds himself compelled to do original work at every turn. The pleasure of investigation of this kind is very real," he added, not least because in no other profession "is it easier to for a man to make his life count." Forestry was unusual in the rigorous challenges it offered and the unique chance it provided to serve the nation—"in few other professions can a man lead so useful a life." Those who heard Pinchot apparently could not resist his missionary-like zeal.[16]

Count the nineteen-year-old Koch among them. He, too, had a conversion experience that summer, for Pinchot visited the student assistants' camp in Washington State. "I was much impressed with his magnetic personality and enthusiasm," Koch recalled, "and he took an individual interest in each of the young men in the party." Although he did not record the specifics of his conversations with Pinchot, Koch's subsequent actions speak volumes about what had transpired that summer in the Pacific Northwest forests. Once he returned to Bozeman to begin his junior year, Koch began preparing for his graduate studies. He knew that the Pinchot family was in the process of underwriting the founding of the Yale Forest School, which opened its doors in 1900: "By this time I had pretty well made up my mind that I wanted to be a forester, and here was my opportunity. I must go to Yale."[17]

He went, loved his studies in the classroom and the field, made countless friends with whom he would work for the rest of his life, and reveled in the camaraderie they developed. To wit, during the two alumni weekends Koch experienced while in New Haven, the forestry students donned "Lincoln green costumes, assembled around a great oaken table in one of the ancient oak-paneled student dining rooms, quaffed our nut brown ale, and sang our songs, and felt we were very close to Sherwood Forest."[18]

That legendary English woodland hardly compared to the size or scope of the forests in the western United States to which the Forest Service assigned Koch following his graduation and successful completion of the Bureau of Forestry's civil service exam. With his master's degree in hand, in the summer of 1903 Koch reported to the agency's small upper-floor office in the nation's capital. Within a matter of days, he was on a train to California. His assignment was to survey, mark, and map the boundaries of any remaining timbered acres that the government still owned surrounding Mount Shasta. That summer and fall, Koch rode up and down the region surrounding the snow-clad peak; corrected the inaccurate and "thoroughly scandalous and fraudulent maps" that the General Land Office in the Department of Interior had constructed years earlier; and by the time cooler weather settled over the region, could report that he had "the Shasta country all on my maps."[19] These served as the basis for the reserve's establishing proclamation. It was a happy day when that document arrived "back from the White House, freshly signed by President Roosevelt, with the boundaries just as I had drawn them on my maps. I felt as though I had given birth to a baby."[20]

Boundary work remained Koch's pride and joy. For the next two years, he and his colleagues crisscrossed the west. They endured the long and grueling hours in the saddle, and, in the process, "polished a lot of leather." These men were as diligent in tracking obscure landownership details in county courthouses and surveyors' offices, data gathering that was critical to legitimizing the ever-expanding number of forest reserves. Their expansion into the national forest system, for all the benefits that may have accrued, came at huge loss for Native Americans. Historian Theodore Catton, among others, has demonstrated that the government's capacity to set aside the national forests, and later to protect some of these lands as wilderness, depended on removing tribal claims and erasing treaty guarantees and reservation boundaries so that the Forest Service could control these forests and grasslands. President Theodore Roosevelt and forester Gifford Pinchot were particularly complicit in this dispossession, a disturbing legacy that still troubles relations between tribes and the federal agency.[21]

Koch makes no mention of this disturbing reality, instead concentrating on the ratcheting up of his workload and responsibilities resulting in the 1905 establishment of the Forest Service. He was among those whom Pinchot "pitchforked" into a newly defined job of forest inspector. Their work came with the heady charge and heavy obligation to evaluate all current rangers, clear away the deadwood, and test those eager to join the agency as the first generation of American foresters; Elers's descriptions of the examinations, written and practical, constitute some of the funniest passages in *Forty Years a Forester*. Koch was thrilled that Pinchot tapped him to serve as the inspector in Montana and Idaho and quickly set up his headquarters in his hometown of Bozeman. As important was his succeeding assignment—to evaluate the Lewis and Clark South Forest Reserve, a job that led Koch to roam across "a vast area of wilderness country" running along the Blackfoot, Swan, Flathead and Sun Rivers. These wildlands would figure significantly in his later work for the agency and in his professional articles about land management principles, prospects, and problems.[22]

These treks' physical challenges added to their pleasure. A muscular masculinity permeates Koch's memories of these years and is especially evident in his post-career novel, *The High Trail*. In this tale of survival keyed to young adult readers, the protagonists set out to cross the Continental Divide before winter sets in, but they fail to do so when frigid weather and blinding snow trap them in the remote, fierce, and unforgiving terrain. Living by their wits and struggling against all odds (as well as some ferocious wolves), they manage to make it to the next spring; in Koch's hands, theirs is a story as harrowing as the landscape itself. Much like his characters, whose hardships in some cases mirrored his daunting experiences in those same wildlands, Elers embraced the affective rewards that came from surmounting such life-threatening tests. One such recompense came during a quiet moment when he and some Forest Service colleagues boarded a motorboat that ferried them along the "beautiful thoroughfare between upper and lower Priest Lake in Idaho." As the men gazed out at "the lovely channel, overhung with virgin white pine, cedar, and hemlock, with the evening light on the water," one of Koch's companions turned to him, saying with understated glee: "And to think we are getting paid for this."[23]

Such compensatory delights dovetailed with the agency's mission and Pinchot's galvanizing promise to this first generation of trained rangers—that their work was of paramount importance. That tight fit also accounts for why Koch's memoir hews closely to, and can serve as a parallel narrative of, the Forest Service's first four decades. His strenuous efforts to set the boundaries of new forest reserves was the first of his major contributions to the agency. Koch also played a central role in defining the agency's increasingly aggressive policies to fight fire in the western United States. Then, as now, this was a definitive issue. "The year of a forester in the western districts," he observed, "is divided into two parts—the forest fire season, and the rest of the year."[24] It was so because of the number and size of conflagrations that roared through the northern Rockies region for much of Koch's career; as he put it, "I have lived through at least nine years which could be classed as really bad forest fire years: 1910, 1914, 1917, 1919, 1925, 1926, 1929, 1931, and 1934." The severity of these blazes, and Koch's gripping accounts of these conflagrations, is a singular motif in *Forty Years a Forester*.

During the off season, however, he spent considerable time thinking about how better to respond to these and other exigencies, a set of analyses that led him to develop a series of formal training procedures and much-needed technical innovations. Forester Ben Huey enumerated some of their significance in an article in *Journal of Forestry*, the discipline's most important outlet. Noting that Koch's "genius cropped out in such products as (1) skilled boards of review of fires, (2) pioneering in fixed lookout networks and seen-area maps, (3) an ingenious map orienting table, and (4) a fire tool that bears his name," Huey offered this concluding praise of Koch's impact on the agency and profession. "Fire boss and fire fighter *par excellence*, the Region has had few men to match his skill and stamina."[25]

That might have been legacy enough for anyone, but Koch's formative influence was manifest in other, more regenerative work. This included his role as the driving force behind the establishment of the Savenac Nursery on the Lolo National Forest, a forest for which he served as supervisor. Typically, the multitasking Koch came up with idea for the nursery, which would become the first in the northern Rockies, and for a time the agency's largest, while he and his new wife, Gerda, enjoyed their nuptials by camping in the woods. They had married in December 1906 but had the good sense to delay their outdoor honeymoon until the following summer. During one of their hikes, the newlyweds came upon an abandoned homestead abutting the Savenac River. To Elers's practiced eye, the site was perfect for a tree plantation. The next spring, he oversaw a planting crew that dug seedlings into the warming soil, early growth that within two years would go up in smoke when the furious 1910 fire incinerated three million acres in Idaho and Montana, taking out the nursery and good part of the Lolo National

Forest. Undeterred, Koch and his staff replanted the site, and over the next thirty-five years it would produce upwards of seven million seedlings. Although Koch would later laugh that this good work held a divine implication—"When a forester goes to Saint Peter for a final accounting, I am sure that when he is asked what he has done with his life, if he can point to thousands of acres of once-ugly burn now covered with a growing forest, it will offset many sins of omission and commission"—his joke contained a serious claim. Landscape restoration was critical to the agency's mission.[26]

A more earthly set of judgments about Koch's abilities came whenever his career hit a new milestone. His twenty-fifth year with the Forest Service in 1928 brought a wave of testimonials bearing witness to his manifold accomplishments. Henry Graves, who had been dean of the Yale Forest School when Koch studied there and had also supervised his work while serving as the agency's second chief from 1910 to 1920, was lavish in his praise. "Elers Koch has attained a distinctive place in the profession," Graves wrote, due to his "ability to cut to the heart of a problem, with clarity of perception that reveals an unusual quality of mind." His keen insights, when combined with "his powers of analysis, his objective viewpoint, [and] his understanding of realities, have enabled him to lay solid foundations of silviculture and forest management in the region in which he has devoted many years of untiring effort and deep study."[27]

One of Koch's contemporaries, Ferdinand Silcox, who later served as chief from 1933 to 1939, waxed nostalgic about their shared labor in the "boundary gang." Perhaps the most entertaining part of their work came when the men then reunited in Washington DC after a tough field season. By day, they juggled "G.L.O. maps to frame up proclamations for T.R to sign." By night, they repaired to the Century Club "for Chianti and battle pool." Even more cherished than what Silcox called these halcyon "days of the Empire" was the subsequent time the two men shared in Missoula, helping manage District One (now known as Region 1), a territory that today encompasses 25 million acres of forests and grasslands spread across Montana, Idaho, and parts of the Dakotas.

"From the store of your seasoned experience," Silcox mused, "your calm judgment and your high hopes of realization you gave to us all associated with you most generously."[28] However awkwardly expressed, Silcox's sentiment was as clear as Raphael Zon's was direct. "You and I hardly agree on anything," wrote the head of the Forest Service's Lakes States Forest Experiment Station, "and yet I like your ideas and profited many a time by your incisive criticism." Zon's critical embrace of his colleague ended on a similarly complex note: "Many Kochs in the Service would be disastrous, but one Koch, and there is no one like you, is a blessing. We want that blessing to last forever."[29]

Koch's career would not last that long, of course. Yet, in a certain sense, it did. He trained so many young foresters, mentored and guided them through one fire season after another, and educated others through his professional articles and public lectures that he helped pave the way for some of their future achievements. They knew how much they owed him and repaid him by learning to think as rigorously and to work as hard. One of those admiring protégés was Robert (Bob) Marshall.[30] Known as the Rocky Mountain Greyhound for the blistering pace he set while shouldering seventy-pound packs on an uphill hike (the steeper the grade the better), Marshall, like Koch, loved wild country. His ambition to protect it from despoliation led him to advocate for wilderness inside and outside the agency, in time becoming one of the founders and financial patrons of the Wilderness Society in 1935. Although he would die but four years after the organization's creation, so crucial were Marshall's contributions to the movement and so abiding was his love for the pristine mountains of western Montana where he had once worked that following the passage of the Wilderness Act in 1964, one of the first designations was of the Bob Marshall Wilderness Area. Dubbed "the Bob," this sprawling terrain covers roughly one million acres along the Continental Divide, and each of the four national forests that administers portions of it have one thing in common: Elers Koch had a hand in surveying, establishing, and administering them. How apt, then, that Marshall helped organize a 1928 dinner in Missoula honoring Koch's silver anniversary in the Forest Service. Fitting too were the words Marshall inscribed in Koch's copy of *The People's Forest* (1933), Marshall's powerful defense of the national forest system:

> To Elers Koch, an advocate of public ownership of land long before I could even tell a white pine from a curly hemlock, and also one of the important reasons why the Forest Service has demonstrated the desirability of public management by its own 28 year old career.[31]

It must have been difficult for Koch to step away from a profession that had been so closely aligned with his personal affinities and aspirations. J. N. Templer, then-supervisor of the Deerlodge National Forest, chose to accent the positive in his congratulatory letter: "You have succeeded in your chosen profession, raised three fine boys and inspired many budding foresters with determination and zeal to make good." The rest and relaxation that would come now that this work was over would have multiple rewards, Templer asserted: "One can freely indulge his hobbies in the daytime and during those small hours of the night . . . one can recall, see and again experience the highlights of the past . . . in short, a springtime in the fall."[32]

Despite Templer's clever phrasing—"a springtime in the fall"—his words read as if Koch was being turned out to pasture. Harry Gisborne, director of the Northern Rocky Mountain Forest and Range Experiment Station, would have none of that, urging Koch to do what he had always done: "Your biographer will find that you have consistently looked over the whole field of forestry in this region, picked out THE one feature most in need of remedy or improvement, and then applied yourself to that job until you saw it done." He then tasked his colleague to apply that same approach to a considered and much-needed assessment of the agency's future. Show "us how we got to where we are, and then [offer] one final selection of 'Here is the next vital issue.' What do you pick, this time, for *us* to push and pull and dig and work and fight for?"[33]

Forty Years a Forester, as a record of Koch's professional engagement and of the evolution of his thoughts about forests, foresters, and forestry, is in no small part a response to Gisborne's plea. It records as well

Koch's perceptions of what constitutes a well-lived life. He continued to tramp the woods he knew intimately, to scale mountains that he had yet to climb, to "go all out." There was nothing retiring about Koch's bounding backwoods energy, a contemporary noted in the 1930s. "More than any one person, Elers Koch characterizes Missoula's skillful merger of outdoors and indoors. This gnarled and wizened man was not too old a decade ago to lead the first successful ascent of the sheer tusk of Granite Peak," which, at 12,087 feet, was the state's tallest mountain; advancing age had not crippled his ability to "follow a woodland trail that would thwart a lynx."[34]

Koch tracked Lewis and Clark just as tirelessly, albeit from his post-retirement desk, writing a series of historical essays about their intrepid journey through the northern Rockies in the first decade of the nineteenth century.[35] By tracing their trails and travails, he also carried forward his father's fascination with Lewis and Clark's legendary leadership of the Corps of Discovery Expedition. Peter Koch's western Americana library, his son remembered proudly, was "one of the best in the West and included many rare first editions of early western journals," a cache that over time Elers would expand. At its inception, this repository, and the knowledge it contained, was a lure for the many scholars who spent time in the elder Koch's home in Bozeman. One of them, historian Elliot Coues, came away from a Peter Koch–led outing to Bozeman Pass with a more refined understanding of Clark's route over that same windswept footpath. Likewise, Elers's careful scholarship and groaning bookshelves tutored a host of literary and academic writers. Ivan Doig's novel, *English Creek*—like Norman Maclean's *Young Men and Fire*, Bernard DeVoto's *The Course of Empire*, and Stephen J. Pyne's *Year of the Fires: The Story of the Great Fires of 1910*—depended on and paid homage to Koch's pathbreaking work in the woods and in his study. In different ways, they each adopted Koch's use of the past to caution the present about its future.[36]

As robust as Koch's post-agency career was, as captivating as his research findings proved to be, a mounting series of personal blows took a toll. His beloved wife Gerda died in 1942 after a long struggle with cancer, and her death may have precipitated his retirement the next year. World War II added to Elers's distress. His three sons enlisted in the U.S. armed forces: Stanley served in the Navy, and Thomas was a navigator in the U.S. Army Air Corps, the same branch that Peter joined, flying transport planes in the China-Burma-India Theater. Stanley's death in 1944, during the Normandy invasion, compounded Elers's grief.

There were literary disappointments too. He could not find a publisher for *Forty Years a Forester*, which he completed in 1949; the manuscript would not see the light of day for nearly fifty years after he completed it. By his seventieth birthday in 1950, Koch's body was also wearing down. Once preternaturally active and renowned for his "agility, toughness, and determination," he now suffered "insupportable pain and immobility from sciatica and arthritis," a diminution of strength and control that seemed insufferable. In 1954, Elers Koch, whose family, friends, and colleagues knew how much he valued being self-sufficient, would die on his own terms, by his own hand.[37]

Years earlier, Koch had foreshadowed the sense of decline, of a last act closing that ultimately would lead him to take his own life. This foreboding sensibility haunts what may be his finest essay, "The Passing of the Lolo Trail." Originally published in the *Journal of Forestry* in 1935, and properly serving as the final chapter of *Forty Years a Forester*, it dissects what Koch believed were the reasons for the demise of the wild, a death that was physical and cultural, literal and metaphorical. He packed these disparate elements into the essay's first paragraph. "The Lolo Trail is no more," Koch declared. "The bulldozer blade has ripped out the hoof tracks of Chief Joseph's ponies. The trail was worn deep by centuries of Nez Perce and Blackfeet Indians, by Lewis and Clark, by companies of Northwest fur traders, by General Howard's cavalry horses, by Captain Mullen, the engineer, and by the early-day forest ranger. It is gone, and in its place there is only the print of the automobile tire in the dust." Modernity and its engines had overrun the wild. Modernity and its comforts had displaced the primordial pressures that once animated white settler colonists who had carved their livelihoods out of this primeval land.[38]

FIG. 4. Elers Koch, sitting in front of his prized Bodmer Atlas, shortly before his death in 1954; pain from sciatica and arthritis had taken its toll. Photo by I. Eide.

No institution was more responsible for this damage than Koch's employer, the U.S. Forest Service. The agency "sounded the note of progress," to which a younger Koch had responded eagerly and with alacrity. Toward the end of his career, however, that siren call had become a dirge as the agency, bent on controlling the natural world, penetrated deeper into unmapped territories. It "opened up the wilderness with roads and telephone lines, and airplane landing fields. It capped the mountain peaks with white-painted lookout houses, laced the ridges and streams with a network of trails and telephone lines, and poured thousands of firefighters year after year in a vain attempt to control forest fires." This reality—in which Koch was implicated—compelled him to ask a tough question of his colleagues' (and his own) faith in the rightness of their collective impact. "Has all this effort and expenditure of millions of dollars added anything to human good?" He thought not. Putting his ideas into action, Koch proposed a radical retreat, if managed properly, that would reduce expenses and, more importantly, enhance wilderness areas and promote wilderness values. The Forest Service should set aside "a carefully defined unit of about two million acres as a low-value area which does not justify the cost of fire control. Maintain only existing roads and the major trails. Withdraw the entire fire-control organization and retain only a police force of two or three rangers to protect the game and direct recreational use." Doing so would give nature a chance to recover and the Forest Service an opportunity to regain its balance. "If a mistake has been made it is better to recognize it and change the mistaken policy than to plunge blindly ahead because a certain line of action has been started."[39]

Elegiac and forceful, Koch's essay was also unsettling, even disruptive. So much so that Franklin Reed, editor of the *Journal of Forestry*, initially rejected it. Later, when the Forest Service interceded on Koch's behalf, Reed would only agree to publish Koch's paper if it was accompanied by a prefatory warning, rather than an author-generated abstract. Reed wrote the cautionary language, noting that Koch's essay is a "somewhat partisan discussion of an important and controversial question of land use, 'What shall be done with the low-value back country.' The author, who is evidently a wilderness area enthusiast, maintains that the Forest Service has already made a serious mistake in opening the Selway wilderness with roads, and goes so far as to question the worth-whileness of attempting fire control in that country."[40] To hammer home the journal's official disagreement with Koch's analysis, Reed crafted a hard-nosed editorial that rebutted Koch's assertions that wilderness and recreation were among the national forests' vital resources. He also commissioned an article that he placed immediately following "The Passing of the Lolo Trail." Its title—"The Opposite Point of View"—signaled its countering purpose and neutralizing intent.[41]

There is a delicious irony in that Koch, not Reed, would have the last word. In 1936, one year after Koch published his appeal for wildland preservation, the Forest Service designated the Selway-Bitterroot Primitive Area, a 1.8 million-acre swath that Koch knew intimately.[42] The Wilderness Act of 1964 posthumously affirmed Koch's bracing critique and clarifying vision. The new law required the Forest Service, the National Park Service, and the other federal land management agencies to establish exactly the kind of pristine preserves that Koch had advocated. "A wilderness, in contrast with those areas where man and his own works dominate the landscape," the legislation declared, "is hereby recognized as an area where the earth and its community of life are untrammeled by man, where man himself is a visitor who does not remain."[43] Its enabling language turned Elers Koch's elegy into prophesy.

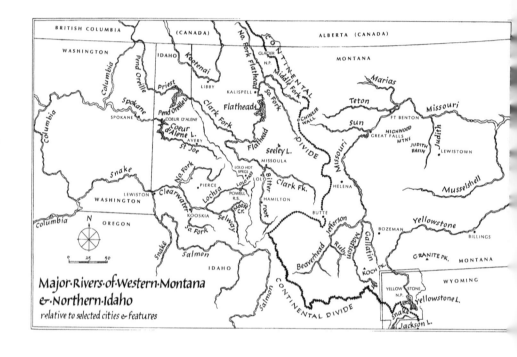

FIG. 5. Map of major rivers of western Montana and northern Idaho.

CHAPTER 1

Montana Boy

I think I was born to be a forester—the profession of forestry in the United States opened up just in time to offer me the kind of life and work that fit my desires and upbringing.

My father, Peter Koch, was one of the pioneers of Montana.[1] He was born in Denmark with the tradition of three or four generations of Lutheran ministers back of him. His father, pastor at Kirkeby, filled the old parsonage with a brood of fifteen children, but somehow or another, in spite of the low income of a country minister, managed to put all of the boys through Latin School and the University.

My father at the age of twenty-one had no expectation other than to take his degree in philosophy at the University of Copenhagen, and carry on the tradition of his family as one more in a line of ministers. But somewhere in the young student was a streak of restlessness. Perhaps the genes of some forgotten Viking ancestor had somewhere infiltrated the sober lineage of the family. At any rate, on a sudden impulse he left the university and took ship to the United States to seek his fortune. After a couple of bitter and unsuccessful years of knocking about the eastern states, the young man ended up at "Bogue Homa," the farm of his uncle in Mississippi. Old Christian Koch, after many years at sea as a ship captain, had found port in southern Mississippi, where he built himself a low, rambling farmhouse, shaded by giant live oaks and imbedded in the flowers that all Kochs love. Here he married a Spanish-French girl, and proceeded to raise a family of twelve children. Welcomed into the family, young Peter fell in love with his shy, dark-haired cousin Laurentze.

But Mississippi, after the Civil War, seemed to offer little opportunity, and Peter decided to go West to better his condition. A loading steamboat at St. Louis caught his eye with a sign, "Ho for Fort Benton and the gold mines." He embarked on the river steamer, and after one hundred days on the Missouri River, delayed by sand bars and snags, he was still one hundred miles short of his destination, Fort Benton.[2]

Again acting on the impulse of the moment he left the boat at Fort Musselshell, an isolated Indian trading post, in what is now Montana. Here he spent the winter of 1869 and 1870, and the following summer, part of the time as a clerk in Clendenning's trading post, but most of the time in a lonely cabin on the river, twenty miles below Musselshell, with a rough crew of woodhawks as partners, cutting wood to be sold to the river steamboats the next spring, living on elk and buffalo meat, and learning to use an axe, his Henry rifle always handy to stand off the constantly prowling Sioux. It was here that young Peter entered in his little red diary, "Twenty-five years old today, and still poor as a church rat." The venture proved unsuccessful. The next spring steamboat traffic on the river dropped to a few boats and the Indians eventually burned most of the wood.

Peter decided to look for more promising fields, and took horse for Bozeman, then a small pioneer farming and cattle town.[3] It was five years before he could accumulate enough worldly wealth to go south for his Laurentze.

After a period as clerk in the Crow Indian Reservation post at Absarokee, Nelson Story, one of the pioneer capitalists and entrepreneurs of Bozeman, discovered ability in the young Dane, and gave him charge of an expedition to establish an Indian trading post in the Judith Basin, a

FIG. 6. An early photograph of Peter Koch, Elers' father, undated.

FIG. 7. Koch family portrait, Bozeman, Montana, circa 1900. *On porch, left to right:* an unidentified guest, Laurentze Marie Koch, and Lucie Koch. *Ground level, left to right:* Elers Koch, Annette Netto Koch, Stanley Koch. *On stairs:* Peter Gyllembourg Koch.

wild and unsettled country, inhabited only by Indians and a few hide hunters.[4] By now, Peter was getting to be something of a frontiersman. He could take a hand with an axe in the building of the log trading post, kill and butcher his buffalo or elk, or take a rifle shot at the constantly threatening Indians. He even acquired an Indian name: *Massa-chela-shena-hathat*, the "yellow-haired white man," the Crows called him.

But in that rough life he did not forget that he was a man of scholarship. He studied the geology and botany of the country, made maps, and daily entered the weather data in his journal. He even wrote several sketches from the Judith Basin to the pioneer newspaper in Bozeman, the *Avant Courier*.[5]

But Story sold the trading post and Peter returned to Bozeman, where for the next year he worked in Willson's store, studied surveying, and took a public land surveying contract. It was not until 1874 that he felt his future sufficiently secure to go south and bring home his bride.[6]

With such a pioneer background, and living in what was still a very small and primitive western town, it is natural that I grew up with a love for the mountains and the range and outdoor life. Father's affairs gradually prospered, and he became cashier and vice president of the Bozeman National Bank, and began to take his place as a well-known and prominent citizen of Bozeman.

As a growing boy, most of the life of myself and my younger brother, Stanley, centered about the outdoors.[7] A cousin of my parents, Richard Biering, had two ranches within a few miles of town, and we had the run of these to our hearts' content.[8] A Saturday was never satisfactory, winter or summer, when we did not get out to the ranch or take our .22 rifles and a lunch for an all-day walk or ride into one of the canyons or over the hills.

Through the summer, when school was out, horses were our main interest. We of course had a barn back of the house where the old family driving mare, Kate, was stabled, as well as our ponies. After these many years it is strange how I remember the individuality of each of our many horses—much better than I recall the people of the period. We rode, under the direction of cousin Richard, from the time we were so small that we had to be strapped on the horse. Our first pony, which my brother and I usually rode double, was an old cayuse roan named Mary. She was supposed to be twenty-one years old, and strangely enough never got any older; she was always twenty-one. I shall never forget, as a small boy, the first time I got the courage to spur and whip old Mary into what we called a "dead run." The speed and power of the horse's muscles under me thrilled me beyond description.

As we grew up, we had a succession of horses as they might be spared from Richard's ranch, mostly mares. There was Dolly, another roan mare, who had a disagreeable habit of biting when we tightened the saddle cinch, and a horse can bite mighty hard. When she had her colt she could be approached on a picket rope only with a club in hand, as she came at us with ears laid back and teeth bared; but once she was saddled she was as gentle as a dog. There was Peggy, a blue roan, who had a pretty trick of balking at unexpected moments, and often would have to be worked with for an hour before she would consent to go. Then there was old Betsy, a gaunt, tall, bay thoroughbred mare. Perched on her I must have looked like a monkey on a stick, but how she could run! None of the other boys' ponies could keep near her. Only I couldn't stop her when she started running, and had to let her run it out.

Our first ponies that we really owned were Billy, Stanley's horse, and my little brown mare, Belle. They were full sister and brother, bred from a cayuse mare by a Hambletonian stallion. Belle was a splendid little saddle horse, and we understood each other perfectly. From a walk it took only the slightest lift of the reins and a slight lean forward for her to break into a lope. Of course Stanley and I raced all the time. His Billy could never beat my Belle, but he never gave up. Every time we came down Babcock Street toward our house we broke into a race, until the town marshal came to Father and put a stop to it.

As we became older, we became more ambitious as to our mounts. Once cousin Richard left in our corral, for some reason, an unbroken horse he called Slivers. When he was first roped and snubbed to a corral post he fought so hard he battered his head against the post until it was covered with scars. I was alone in the house one day and went out and looked him over. I dropped my rope over him and managed to get my hand on him, and concluded he was not so wild. So I got a halter on him, and worked him over with a saddle blanket till he quit trembling. I put the saddle on and led him out in the street beside the house, and eased myself into the saddle. He didn't buck as hard as I expected, and I stayed with him, and from then on for that summer he was my horse. That was the first completely unbroken horse I had tackled, and I felt pretty proud.

Stanley's best horse was a black gelding . . .⁹ There was a sale of J N horses over at Livingstone, and Stanley went over with some of Richard's hands and bought him. He was a flathipped, rawboned animal, but the most enduring horse I ever rode; no day was too long for him, and he always came in with his head up. But he had one fault. He had been spoiled in breaking, and developed into a bad runaway. When we got him his tongue was cut half in two by the use of a spade bit, and he hated the curb. He might be going along quietly, and suddenly with a powerful lunge he was away on an uncontrolled run, and he ran wild, regardless of obstacles. He fell once with my brother and broke his collarbone; another time, with one of Richard's men, he ran square into a barbwire fence and broke the man's arm. Twice in running horses he got away from me and fell end over end. When Stanley went off to West Point, [his horse] fell to me. I decided I could cure him of running away. It was fighting the curb bit that enraged him, so one day I took him out with a plain bar bit instead of a curb. When we got out to the edge of town, [he] made one of his characteristic lunges and was off. I didn't try to stop him, just kept a steady rein on him, and after he had run five miles he commenced to slow down. Then it was my turn, and I spurred him on till he had all the running he wanted. That was the last time he ever ran away, and from then on anyone could ride him. But that was when I was almost a young man; it is the horses of my boyhood that most come back to me.

From the time I was seven or eight years old, my father used to take the full month of August as vacation from the bank, and the whole family went camping. At first we set up a fixed camp in one of the canyons and stayed in one place, but as my brother and I got older and could look after the horses and the camp work we extended our excursions. Our favorite camping spot was on the Gallatin River, after a wagon road was finally built through the canyon. We usually made three camps during the month, and fished, rode, hunted, and climbed mountains. These summer camps were the high spot of the year. Occasionally we varied the program with a longer trip, once through Yellowstone Park, two or three families together, with a four-horse grub wagon, buggies and saddle horses, a teamster and a Chinese cook. It took a whole month to make a circuit of the park from Bozeman. Nowadays they drive through with a car in a single day, but we saw the park in a way that few people do now.

As we grew into our teens, my brother and I, with a few of our friends, used to take long trips by ourselves with our saddle horses and a pack horse or two, exploring the wonderful country around the Gallatin Valley. We had the greatest of freedom, and our parents never objected to any sort of an expedition we wanted to undertake. Conservative people occasionally asked my father whether he was not worried about such young boys going off alone into the mountains, but he always said he felt they were far safer there than loafing about the pool halls in town. To this day I have never learned to play pool or billiards, which I sometimes think detracts from a well-rounded education, but the mountain training doubtless was far better for us.

The most extensive trip we made was in August 1897. Father was then closely connected with the college at Bozeman,[10] and a semi-scientific expedition was organized to traverse and explore some of the little-known country in Montana and Wyoming, and Yellowstone Park. In addition to my father, there were three members of the college faculty, a Presbyterian minister from Helena, my brother, Stanley, and myself, who were then fifteen and sixteen years old. We, of course, had a saddle horse apiece, and a pack string of seven horses, with Ed Alderson, an old-time mountain man, as packer. The cook, Jim Trail, completed the party.

Ed pitched his tent in what was known as the Alderson pasture at the end of Black Street, and we assembled the outfit there: bedrolls, tents, war bags, and food supplies for a month's trip. My brother and I,

FIG. 8. Peter Koch tending campfire, late 1880s.

excited and wild to be off, slept the night at Ed's camp, and after the usual delay in packing up the first morning, we were off. We struck east from Bozeman over the historic Bozeman Pass, up the Boulder River, past the abandoned mining camp of Cooke City, into Wyoming via the Clark Fork, and up Crandall Creek into Yellowstone Park. At that time, it was an almost uninhabited wilderness. Except for a few old prospectors still hanging on in Cooke City, we saw no one during three weeks of riding. Of course it was outside of hunting season, but both my brother and I carried rifles on our saddles, and riding up the Boulder River we had a chance to use them. A she black bear with two cubs, one black and one brown, were feeding in a huckleberry patch along the trail. Stanley and I were off our horses in a moment, and as the old bear reared up on her hind legs we both fired and she dropped. The cubs climbed high in a lodgepole pine tree, and much excited we continued bombarding till they both were down. We took the hides, which were not good at that time of year, and only served in later years for our dogs to sleep on, and the cubs' hindquarters, which were very good when Jim Trail baked them in the Dutch oven. Dr. Wilcox took the skulls as a contribution to his biology department.[11] Fifty years later I was going through the college buildings as a member of the governor's Post War Planning Commission. I passed what went for a museum, but which was neglected and I hope only temporarily disorganized. I said to the professor escorting me, "I want to go in here and see if I can find something." Sure enough, I ran across three bear skulls, an adult and two cubs, unlabeled and unknown, but doubtless our trophy.

It was a wonderful trip through some of the most attractive mountain country in the United States. The Clark Fork Valley and the Sunlight Basin in Wyoming, which are now cluttered with dude ranches, were completely untenanted by man. We cut up through Crandall Creek, and into the Hoodoo Basin, where Dr. Traphagen and Stanley, the official photographers of the expedition, got some unique photographs of the grotesque eroded rock formations.[12] By this route we entered Yellowstone Park by a back door, which was quite contrary to official procedure. At that time the park was policed by the army, which had two or three troops of cavalry concentrated at Mammoth Springs, with small detachments scattered over the mail travel routes.[13]

About the time we arrived, the whole park was in an uproar over a stage holdup. The robbers had stopped the whole string of seven or eight stages run by the transportation company, relieved the tourists of all their valuables and money, and disappeared into the forest. As it happened, that day we were approaching the Grand Canyon, which would be our first contact with the usual tourist routes. We had been out three weeks, and by that time were a pretty tough-looking outfit. None of the men had shaved since we started, and we wore rough clothes, much the worse for wear. With the guns on our saddles and our general rugged aspect we looked like anything but a bunch of scientists. When we got within two or three miles of the Grand Canyon a messenger from the military post was out looking for a fishing party of soldiers to get them back and on the trail of the bandits. He took one look at our outfit, wheeled his horse, and galloped back to the canyon station to report that he had seen the stage robbers. A squad of cavalrymen was hastily sent out to meet us, put us under arrest, and moved us into camp under guard.

A hard-boiled old-time sergeant of the regular army was in charge of the Canyon Post. We were brought into his headquarters for an examination. My father appeared first as spokesman for the party. He identified himself as Peter Koch, vice president and director of the Bozeman National Bank, an elder in the Presbyterian Church, and a generally well-known and reputable citizen. Next up was Dr. James Reid, fuming with the indignity of such treatment. He was president of the state college, an ordained minister, and a man accustomed to more respect. Then came Dr. Moore, who was minister of the Presbyterian Church in Helena. Then Dr. Wilcox. He was a great big burly man, dressed very carelessly, with a black stubble of beard, and no stage robber could have better looked the part, but he claimed to be a doctor of philosophy and head of the biology department at the college at Bozeman. The sergeant looked at him incredulously and called the next man, Dr. Traphagen, who was head of the department of geology and chemistry at the college. The doctor was a very gentle, kindly appearing man with big brown eyes and a pointed Vandyke beard. Before he could open his mouth, the old sergeant decided he had had enough. "I suppose you are going to tell me you are Jesus Christ," he bellowed. That broke up the examination, and we were returned to our camp, still under guard. The whole military organization was so upset by the holdup that we were kept there for two days, much to the disgust of the party, except my brother and I, who had the time of our lives swaggering around the hotel grounds and listening to the dudes pointing out the desperate stage robbers. Finally, we got permission to go on to Norris under escort, and there at the end of the telegraph line we managed to convince the military of our identity.

We went over Bighorn Pass and camped at the very head of the Gallatin River.[14] It was our last day in the park, and Ed Alderson slipped out before dawn with his little bay packhorse, Johnny, and returned in an hour or two with the quarters of a yearling elk packed on the horse. It was not the first time Ed had poached in the park, but my father was extremely put out over this law violation. That didn't prevent any of us from enjoying the tender elk steaks Jim Trail cooked for us that evening. We thought we had something coming for our treatment by the park authorities.

My father never did think much of the military organization in the park. In a previous packhorse trip in 1883 he and W. W. Wylie, who later ran a transportation outfit in the park, were making a trip through Yellowstone.[15] They left camp one morning leaving a few coals in their campfire in the midst of a green meadow. My father was always especially careful with fire in the forest, and one of my earliest lessons in woodsmanship was to put out my fire. On this occasion, a squad of soldiers discovered the smoldering fire, trailed down the party, and Father and Wylie were brought to the bar of justice. At that time, the army was judge, jury, and executioner, and Father and Wylie were each fined $100, and no appeal. Father never did get over that, and maybe we had the poached elk coming to us.

My father was a scientist of no mean ability. Every day when he came home from the bank, he took the maximum and minimum thermometer readings of the day and thus established the oldest continuous weather record kept in the state. He was well read in geology and an enthusiastic botanist, making a very extensive collection of Montana flora. Naturally we boys absorbed much of it from him. To this day the greater number of Latin names I carry in my mind for plants are the ones I learned from my father. It is just as easy for a boy to learn that a plant is called *mertensia* or *Douglasii* as to call it blue bell or pink moss.

Father was a man of great distinction and dignity in appearance. Some people were afraid of him, but he was really the kindest man in the world, with a little twinkle in his blue eyes at times, though he could be stern when necessary. It was characteristic of the man that even through his

FIG. 9. The 11,286-foot Koch Peak (*left*) in the Madison Range, Montana, is named for Peter Koch.

pioneer days he never became "Pete" to his associates. If anyone called him "Pete" he simply said, "My name is Peter," and that is the way it stayed. The house was full of books, which father gradually collected, the best of the classics, scientific works, biography, and history. His library of western Americana, which I still have, was one of the best in the West and included many rare first editions of early western journals.

As a result of his learning and interest in scientific and historical subjects, many men of distinction from Washington D C and elsewhere who were passing through Bozeman came to Father, and we often had such visitors as guests for dinner. The U.S. Geological Survey men working in the vicinity were all well-known visitors, and we used sometimes to visit them in camp. We had for dinner such men as Elliot Coues, the eminent naturalist and historian, while he was working on his monumental edition of the Lewis and Clark journals.[16] Father drove him over Bozeman Pass, and set him right on a question of the route of Clark over the pass.

There was Olin Wheeler, also working on the Lewis and Clark travels, and Col. Hiram Chittenden, who was then engaged in his fine *History of the American Fur Trade*.[17] I greatly prize the autographed copies of the books of these men, which they presented to Father.

The beginnings of the Montana State College at Bozeman in the early nineties was one of Father's greatest interests. He served for years on the state college board and was greatly influential in shaping the young institution. It was even said that Peter Koch had more influence in the selection of the faculty than the president of the college. Father was particularly proud of the way that the establishment of the local college brought higher education to many Montana boys and girls who never otherwise would have had the opportunity for schooling beyond high school. When I attained college age, naturally I attended the local college rather than going east. Father believed in a broad general education before specializing and helped me select a course which included botany, biology, chemistry, surveying, mathematics, Latin, German, English, history, and philosophy. Since the early classes were very small (there were only six in my graduating class of 1901), we had the advantage of much individual instruction from the heads of departments, which included many notable men, and doubtless got much better instruction than in one of the older and larger colleges.

Among the faculty was Lt. George P. Ahern, detailed from the army as a military instructor. Lt. Ahern, who later became head of the Philippine Forest Service and a distinguished forester, had traveled some with Gifford Pinchot, and had become interested in forestry.[18] I believe it was largely on a suggestion by my father that Ahern, in 1898, offered some lectures on forestry at the state college, the first regular course in forestry given in the United States.[19] However new the subject of forestry might be in this country, it was nothing new to Father. One of his brothers and other relatives were foresters in Denmark. As he thought I might be interested in the subject, which was in line with the scientific work I was taking at the college, I attended Ahern's lectures and took a couple of field excursions with him in the winter woods. About that time Gifford Pinchot had taken over the Bureau of Forestry and was beginning some research in American forests.[20] In the summer of 1899, through the good offices of Lt. Ahern, I got a job as a student assistant in the Bureau of Forestry at $30 a month.

I reported for duty at Tacoma, my first long trip away from home, and we moved immediately to a camp in the woods near a big logging camp where it was arranged for us to board.

There were about twenty men in the crew, most of them Harvard, Yale, or Princeton men who had been influenced by Gifford Pinchot to try this new forestry thing. It was a new and enlightening experience for a raw youngster of eighteen, brought up in a small western town, to come up against these sophisticated, eastern college students, many of them from distinguished families.

There were Bill and Henry James, sons of the famous psychologist William James; Stewart Hotchkiss, scion of one of the oldest New Haven families; Dick Fisher, who later became dean of the Harvard Forestry School, and several such men as Alfred Gaskill, E. T. Allen, Tom Sherrard, John Foley, and Bill Hodge, who later took high places in forestry. I got along fine with them in spite of the fact that I was almost the only western man in the party. They knew a lot of things I didn't, but

I knew how to get around in the woods better than they did. Around the campfire I heard all the college songs of the period and made many good friends. It was then that I first met Gifford Pinchot, who spent several days with us in camp. I was much impressed with his magnetic personality and enthusiasm, and he took an individual interest in each one of the young men in the party.

The object of the crew was to study the coastal Douglas-fir forest to determine volume, stand per acre, and rate of growth. We had strenuous but tremendously interesting days working in the great forests of Douglas-fir, hemlock, and cedar. It was hard work running a compass line through devil club and salmonberry, and climbing windfalls higher than a man's head, but I loved it. Toward the end of the season, we moved up into what is now Mount Rainier National Park and got to see some of the glaciers and snowfields of the great mountain which always towered over us.[21] It was a thoroughly satisfactory summer, and I came home with $60 in my pocket for two months' work, which was more cash than I had ever had, and enough to buy the shotgun I had been wanting.

A year before I took my bachelor's degree in Bozeman, the Yale School of Forestry, a graduate school, was started under the auspices of Gifford Pinchot, and with his close friend and associate, Henry S. Graves, as dean.[22] By this time I had pretty well made up my mind that I wanted to be a forester, and here was the opportunity. I must go to Yale.

My journey to New Haven was my first trip east. At the present time there is no great difference between the students of western colleges and those of the big eastern universities. They wear the same kind of clothes, read the same things, and talk the same language. It was quite different forty-seven years ago.

As an inexperienced raw western boy of twenty, I fell into a strange country. At least at first impression, the students looked and acted very differently from my small town associates. That was a period when young men wore very wide peg-top trousers and very short jackets. Such a fashion had never penetrated to Montana. The first thing I did was to go to a tailor and order two suits just as wide in the trousers and short in the coat as the rest of them. At least I could go that far in becoming

FIG. 10. Elers Koch, 1901.

FIG. 11. Yale Forest School graduate students, 1902.

a Yale student. I was fortunate in getting in with a group of very fine fellows, all of whom afterwards entered the Forest Service and attained prominent places. There were A. W. Cooper and W. D. Sterrett, both Harvard graduates, J. G. Peters from Johns Hopkins, and Theodore Salisbury Woolsey Jr. from Yale. They had a good deal of fun with the wild man from Montana, but I soon learned to smoke a pipe, and to know the difference between a Manhattan and a martini, and superficially, at any rate, became civilized.

The faculty of the forest school was small, and so were the classes, so we had close individual contact with our professors. Henry S. Graves, the dean, was a man of the highest ability and distinction and a good teacher. There were practically no American textbooks in forestry at that time, so we had to use European ones, mostly English. Schlich's *Manual of Forestry*,[23] in five volumes, was our standby, though we tried hard to wade through Gayer's *Waldbau* in German.[24] At any rate, we learned the elements of forestry, silviculture, dendrology, forest management, forest economics, wood technology, surveying, and some of the kindred sciences.

The Yale bicentennial celebration happened to occur the first fall I arrived and gave me a glimpse of undergraduate life. It was a great sight; all the undergraduates were dressed in colonial costumes: Pilgrims, Indians, etc. The Yale School of Forestry students made a hit by appearing in Robin Hood costumes, Lincoln green jerkin, tights, and hood, with bow and arrows slung over our backs.

The old grads loved it. I recall seeing Gifford Pinchot with kindred spirits of his class driving up and down the streets in an open dray, singing at the top of their lungs:

Show me the Scotchman who doesn't love the thistle,
Show me the Englishman who doesn't love the rose.
But show me the true-hearted son of old Eli
Who doesn't love the spot-one-two-three [business of beating the
     breast],
Whe-e-ere the elm tree grows.

And all this without benefit of external stimulant, at least on the part of G.P. So far as I ever heard he never took a drink.

Taft's class[25] was also there in force, singing lustily,

It's a great class, an up-to-date class
Seventy eventy eventy eventy eight.

I can't remember whether Taft himself took part; perhaps it was not in keeping with the dignity of a chief justice.

The top feature of the day was in the evening when we foresters, still in Lincoln green costumes, assembled around a great oaken table in one of the ancient oak-paneled student dining places, quaffed our nut brown ale, and sang our songs, and felt that we were very close to Sherwood Forest.

The course at Yale lasted two years before I took my degree as master of forestry [in 1903]. The last spring term we spent in field exercises on the large timber tract connected with West Point Military Academy on the Hudson. It is a beautiful country and we had a wonderful time there. My brother, Stanley, was still a cadet there so we had an opportunity to see something of the school. The commanding officer was very obliging and permitted us to use saddle horses from the cadet stables, much to my pleasure at getting into the saddle again.

Shortly before the end of the spring term we all drove down to New-berg to take the Bureau of Forestry civil service examinations. Our whole course had been pointed up for this examination, and naturally we were all considerably worked up over it.

We all finished late in the afternoon. Whether we had passed or not, at least the tension was over and we were all in the mood to celebrate. Woolsey started opening champagne before dinner, and we all gathered around a table in the Newberg Hotel for a hilarious meal. Afterwards we drove home in the moonlight, loudly singing, "By the light of the silvery moon." It was an occasion to reminisce about when I met any of my old classmates, many of whom, alas, are now dead and gone.

CHAPTER 2

Gifford Pinchot's Young Men

We have a favorite story in this region about Dorr Skeels, a graduate of the forest school at Michigan, and one of the early supervisors of the Kootenai Forest.[1] Skeels was a small and rather undistinguished looking man with a sharp wit and a humorous way of talking that was enhanced by his stammer, which I think he exaggerated somewhat for effect.

Skeels was traveling one day on the Great Northern train between Libby and Spokane when a lumberman acquaintance introduced him to a young man, the proud scion of one of the big Northwest lumber families. He was a tall, hulking fellow, who had been a famous guard on one of the Yale football teams, and was properly aware of the importance of himself and his family. He towered over Skeels as he shook hands, and remarked patronizingly, "Oh, you are one of Gifford Pinchot's boys."

Skeels looked up at him, quizzically, and returned, "Ye-ye-yes, I am one of G-G-Gifford Pinchot's boys. Wh-wh-whose boy are you?"

I have always been proud of being one of Gifford Pinchot's young men. It was as fine, enthusiastic, and inspired a group of public employees as was ever assembled. Now, when I arrived in Washington in June

1902, I had, to my satisfaction, an appointment signed by the secretary of agriculture as forest assistant at a salary of $1,000 a year. I found the Bureau of Forestry established in a few dingy rooms in the old Atlantic Building, which was to be the home of the expanding Forest Service for many years.

At that time the Bureau of Forestry contained practically all the trained foresters in the country, but, alas, controlled no forest land to administer. Such forest reserves as had been established were still under control of the General Land Office in the Department of Interior. Mr. Pinchot had been moving heaven and earth, and exerting all his very great influence with President Theodore Roosevelt, to get the reserves transferred to the Department of Agriculture, but so far had succeeded only to the extent of obtaining permission to give the Land Office technical advice.

Acting on this authority, he had organized what we called the Boundary Division under F. E. Olmsted.[2] The best public forest lands were rapidly passing into the hands of the lumber companies through all the devices of the public land laws, homesteads, timber and stone claims, and scrip. There was no time to lose, and G.P. was sending his young men to ride the forests and mountains of all parts of the West, from Canada to Mexico, to map and report on all the considerable bodies of forest land still remaining in public ownership.

Many years later, one summer evening, I was traveling by motorboat with a few other Forest Service men through the beautiful thoroughfare between lower and upper Priest Lake in Idaho.[3] As we lay back on our bedrolls in the boat and slowly wound around the curves of the lovely channel, overhung with virgin white pine, cedar, and hemlock, with the evening light on the water, one of the men turned to me and said, "And just to think we are getting paid for this."

That was the way I felt about my new job. I doubt if there has ever been such a wonderful job in the world as the early day forest boundary work. One was given a state map of say California, or Montana or Wyoming, with an area of a few million acres roughly blocked out in green. One proceeded to the nearest point by rail, and then rode all summer, seeing thrilling new wild country every day, sometimes with a pack outfit and packer, more often riding alone, stopping where night overtook one at small towns, ranches, sheep camps, or mines, or sleeping out if necessary. There was no great amount of burdensome detail; the country was mapped by traverse and from high points, sketching in the various timber types, grassland, barren, and brush. We figured on covering half a township to a township a day, and that is a lot of country.

At the end of the field season, we returned to Washington and took up desks in a big room in the Atlantic Building to prepare our reports and maps, and draw in the boundaries for the new reserves. As fast as completed, proclamations were drawn and dispatched to President Roosevelt, who signed them, and thus added another million or two acres to the growing forest reserves.

I stayed in Washington only a few days—enough to shake hands with Gifford Pinchot, and to get some general instructions from Fritz Olmstead and such maps as were available, and to learn how to submit a government expense account.

My first job was to be the Mt. Shasta area in California. Exultantly I boarded the train. I was going west again. I was awake at daylight at Livingston for the first sight of the Crazy Mountains, that outpost of the Rocky Mountains, the high peaks shining in the morning sun.[4] How good the mountains looked to me! I was back in my home country.

I stopped in Bozeman for a few days to visit with my family, and then on to California. At Redding I met Alfred F. Potter, who had charge of the boundary work in California. Potter was an experienced stockman, formerly secretary of the Arizona Stockmen's Association, whom G.P. had met several years before and persuaded to come into the new Bureau of Forestry as grazing expert.[5] It was a fine example of G.P.'s ability to pick the right man. No longer could the stockmen say the bureau men were only theorists who knew nothing of western ways. Potter could meet them on any ground. He was a rather small, soft-speaking man with a friendly approach, and was a real asset to the young bureau. I liked him right away.

This was my first trip to California, and I reveled in the almost tropical feeling of Redding in the Sacramento Valley, the fresh black figs in the market, the exotic trees and the hot nights. After dinner in the evening everybody in the hotel moved their chairs into the street and sat with their feet on the curb for the extra coolness of the outdoors.

Our first job was in the Land Office, to take off their plats and tract books all the data on land entries, homesteads, timber claims, scrip, and railroad grants, and to copy off the topography from the township plats. The Land Office Register and Receiver showed the usual veiled hostility to the Bureau of Forestry men, but made their records available to us.

The township plat work completed, we took the train to Sisson on the Upper Sacramento River. Sisson was a small lumbering town on the timbered volcanic plateau surrounding Mt. Shasta. I was delighted with the first view of Shasta, that most beautiful of mountains towering in virgin white above the timbered plateau. On the slopes just below timberline were great open fields, and I remarked to Potter what wonderful meadows those must be. He smiled his little smile, and said wait till I see them. Little did I know then of the great California brush fields, products of past forest fires, and almost impenetrable, either afoot or horseback. I was to have many a tough struggle through them.

For lack of anything better to do the first evening we drifted through two or three of the many saloons in the town. I particularly recall a poker game going on in one of the bars between a group of half a dozen lumberjacks and cowpunchers. One man, a gigantic negro, was having a run of bad luck, and regularly every half hour would call for a new deck and dash the old deck to the floor, which was half covered with cards. I don't think it improved his luck much.

Potter rode with me only a couple of days to show me the work, which was quite simple if one had an eye for topography and could sketch in timber types from a vantage point. When he left I was to be on my own until late fall.

Sisson was the center of a rapidly developing lumber industry, and the timber was quite wonderful, giant ponderosa and sugar pines and incense cedar. The timber was so heavy that in places three separate fellings had to be made to get room for the logs to lie on the ground.

I was soon to learn from my township plats that most of the fine timber on the plateau and lower slopes had passed into private ownership. The government still owned the top of Mt. Shasta and the upper white fir slopes above the pine types. I found some pretty good government timber in the rougher topography, but the timber cruisers had not missed much of the cream.

In the course of the summer I reached timberline on Shasta from all sides, and have always regretted that I did not take the opportunity to climb the mountain, but I suppose it is none too good an undertaking for a man alone to tackle the steep snow slopes.

After covering all the country I could from Sisson, I worked down the line of the Southern Pacific, stopping at such small towns as Castella and Lamoine. In those days every town of any size boasted a livery stable, and I was able to hire a saddle horse in most places. At Lamoine the best animal I could get was a little white mule. He was not a bad saddle animal for mountain trails, with an easy ambling gait. One day I had planned an extra-long trip, from the Sacramento River by a trail across the range and down to the Trinity River, intending to offset on the Trinity and return by another trail a few miles to the north. It turned out to be a much longer ride than I had expected, and nightfall found me on the Trinity River in wild and unsettled country. There was no grass for my mule, so I tied the little beast to a tree and equally supperless lay down for the night under my saddle blanket.

I was up at gray of dawn, intending to continue on north as planned, but the little mule had other ideas. Not one step would he move farther from home. I spurred and whipped him, and tried leading him, but finally had to admit defeat and return the same way I had come. About seven o'clock I ran into a hunters' camp and sat down to a welcome breakfast of deer liver and bacon. The hunters were disconsolate. They had started with a gallon jug of whisky, packed in their bedroll for safety, and had rolled a packhorse on a bad bit of trail, breaking the whisky jug in the bedroll. One of them said mournfully they hadn't had a drink since they started, but went to bed sober every night and woke up drunk.

As I worked farther down the Sacramento River, I gradually came into a new and fascinating type of country—foothills covered with oak and

FIG. 12. Elers Koch ready to ride.

digger pine.[6] The farther down the valley I got the hotter it grew. I rode all day, many times with the thermometer at 115°F. At that temperature one never rode a horse off the walk or slow jog trot, but as the air was dry I rather enjoyed the heat.

There were two new things I learned about riding in the California country. One was the block sulphur matches that seemed to be peculiar to that country. One broke a sliver off the block, scratched it on one's pants, and then waited half a minute while the thing sputtered and smelled before it burst into flame. A small block one could put in the shirt pocket sufficed to light the brown paper cigarettes for a week. I guess they don't make them anymore. The other thing was the fact that they didn't know what oats were in California. They fed the horses rolled barley. I didn't get a feed of oats for my horse all summer.

When I finished the country along the Southern Pacific, I felt the need for a different form of transportation which would take me farther back. So for $35 I bought a horse, a little brown gelding that served me well the rest of the summer.

Some of the country I had to cover on the McCloud River[7] and Squaw Creek[8] was remote from settlements, so I had to look for a pack outfit. I connected up with two brothers, Tom and Jim—I can't recall their last name. They had a small cattle ranch back up Squaw Creek, accessible only by trail, where they cultivated a patch of alfalfa, and ran a couple of hundred head of cattle in the mountains. I engaged Jim for a few weeks, with a pack mule to carry our outfit. He was a fine fellow, and I enjoyed riding with him.

The cattle in that country were interesting. There is practically no grass on their summer ranges in the mountains, and they lived entirely on browse. Either from their feed or the character of the country, they developed into quite different animals from the clumsy cattle of the plains. They were sleek and active, and more like wild game than domestic stock.

The country was different from my Montana mountains. It was drier and sunnier and warmer; this together with the oaks and madronas and the red-barked manzanita, and the sycamores along the streams instead of cottonwoods, gave it to me a strange and exotic character.

The country was full of deer and bear. One day, riding down the McCloud River, the trail all day had been padded down by bear tracks, big and little. That night Jim and I camped on the trail and turned the stock back up the river to graze. In order to prevent the horses from coming down the river I put my bedroll for the night directly in the trail.

I was sound asleep when I was awakened by something seizing my canvas bed tarp and jerking it half off me. As I looked up, there in the moonlight was a great dark animal standing directly over me. For a moment I was frozen with terror, then let out a yell and threw up my arms, and away jumped the little pack mule that had come down to investigate the camp. At least I couldn't have been more scared if it had been a bear.

I rode with Jim a few weeks, and then went on my own again, taking chances for a night's lodging at ranches or sheep camps, or solitary mines. People were hospitable in those days and I generally was a welcome guest. There was always an element of chance on where I might land for the night.

One time I had ridden all day and in the evening arrived at a solitary ranch where I hoped to stay. Nobody home. I rode on down the trail in the gathering dusk hoping for a further possibility. It grew darker and darker, and it looked like lying out for another night. About ten o'clock I saw a dim light and turned in. I got no answer to my knock and opened the door. In the dim, smoky hut, with only the light of the fireplace, were two Chinamen.[9] I couldn't induce them to give me any supper at that hour of the night, but they gave me half an old ragged sougan[10] and told me I could sleep in the barn loft. At least I could get feed for my pony, and I fell asleep listening to him contentedly munching hay. In the morning the Chinamen gave me a good breakfast and sent me on my way. Through the whole summer I never had anyone turn me away.

Most of the Shasta country was theoretically surveyed and platted by contractors for the General Land Office. It was a thoroughly scandalous and fraudulent job. In many townships it was impossible to find a single section corner, and the topography on the plats was so inaccurate that it was obvious that no field surveys had been made, although well-drafted plats were filed, and the survey contract money collected. Fortunately, I had the U.S. Geological Survey quadrangle maps for most of the area, and used them for a base rather than the General Land Office survey plats.

So I rode the summer out, and by late September had finished my allotted area. I had the Shasta country all on my maps, and a new forest reserve was ready to be born.[11]

I took the train to San Francisco for instructions on the next job. There happened to be two other boundary men in town, and I spent a couple of days seeing the old San Francisco as it was before the fire. We bought Japanese prints, dined at the Poodle Dog, and spent hours exploring Chinatown. It was like visiting a foreign country. San Francisco has never been the same since the earthquake and fire.

My next assignment was up in the coastal redwood country, north of Eureka. Someone had discovered that there was a block of public land remaining, and as none of the reserves contained any redwood, Potter was anxious to have it examined before it was filed on.

At that time there was no railroad into Eureka; one either had to go by the coastal steamer or take a one-hundred-mile stage trip. So I took a boat from San Francisco, and was of course frightfully seasick. Crossing the bar into the Eureka Bay was really something, the way the boat would rise on the great rollers, hover for a moment, and then pitch down nose first. It surely did things to my stomach.

At Eureka the Land Office people were, as usual, suspicious and not too friendly. A search of the records disclosed that there was indeed about a half a township of public land left bordering the coast. It was worth looking at. Eureka was primarily a lumber town, and large-scale logging of the giant redwoods was just getting well under way, though there was not yet much of a hole in the vast coastal forest. I rode north two days from Eureka. The narrow dirt road wound leisurely among the vast trunks of the redwoods, now and then emerging on the open fern-covered cliffs above the ocean, with the rollers of the wide Pacific breaking at their base. It was a marvelous ride. I have been over it since on the modern highway. The Save the Redwoods League has done a splendid piece of work in preserving so many fine examples of the virgin redwood, but of course these limited strips cannot give the same effect as the miles and miles of untouched forest I rode through.[12]

Owing to the tremendous size of the timber, redwood logging is about as completely destructive a process as one can imagine. A few years ago I visited a large-scale operation. The logging railroads usually follow the ridges, and the logs are power skidded uphill after the area has been burned over to clear it of some of the logging slash. Standing on such a ridge in the midst of the operation I felt that I was looking at a mining operation rather than a timber job. One might have been standing on the Butte Hill, an equally black and forbidding spot.[13] Donkey engines throb and send up clouds of steam in all directions, while the great logs come crashing up on steel cables, the dust rising from the black burned ground. The size of the timber precludes any manhandling; it is all machine and brute power. I was glad to get away from it all.

Two days' ride brought me to my area. I managed to locate a few section corners, and discovered that the whole area was situated on barren, fern-covered cliff and rocks with practically no timber on it. It was too much to expect that the timber cruisers had overlooked anything good.

I dreaded to take the boat back to San Francisco, and was almost tempted to take a one-hundred-mile stage ride instead, but my pride would not let me, and I had to stand the seasickness once more.

I still had one more job before returning to Washington for the winter—the Santa Monica Mountains, a low range of oak- and chaparral-covered hills overlooking the coast, west of Santa Monica.

I got rather a sorry mount in Santa Monica, then a sleepy little coast town, and rode for a week through the hills, greatly enjoying a type of country completely new to me. I never saw mountain quail so abundant; sometimes a whole hillside would be alive with them as they flushed out of the chaparral like a swarm of bees. At one Mexican ranch where I stayed we had a great platter heaped high with the little birds.

On this trip I got well acquainted with the southern California flea. I don't know which is worse—the bedbugs or the fleas. The former are more disgusting, but the flea bites last longer, particularly if they are on that part of the anatomy exposed to rubbing on the saddle. The last day of the trip was a twenty-mile ride along the beach between the mountains and the ocean. There was no road. This whole oceanfront was owned by the Malibu Ranch and was completely uninhabited.[14] It was a most marvelous ride. The tide was out and the hard white sand of the beach at the water's edge was just right. The oak- and chaparral-covered hills rose at my left, and from the right the slow creamy rollers slid in from the blue Pacific. With his head turned toward home and the sand under his feet my old nag picked up spirits, and could occasionally be spurred into a sharp gallop.

I rode into the Malibu Ranch about six. The owner was not at home, but the foreman kindly fed me and gave me a bed in the walnut house, where I had a final assignment with the ubiquitous fleas.

I have never been back there since, but I understand there is a fine highway along my solitary beach, and the bluffs along the Malibu beach are lined with palatial residences of Hollywood stars. I don't think I want to see it again. I would rather have my memory.

The field season over, we boundary men all assembled in Washington in the late fall, where a dozen of us worked in one big room in the Atlantic Building. Base maps were drafted from all available data, the forest types colored in with crayons, and a detailed report made for each township.

The final process was to outline the boundaries of the new reserve and give it a name. The romantic souls of the young men of the boundary survey reveled in such resounding western names as Coconino, Sangre de Christo, Umpqua, Seven Devils, Uncompagre, Hellgate.

When the new proclamation for the Shasta Forest Reserve came back from the White House, freshly signed by President Roosevelt, with the boundaries just as I had drawn them on my maps, I felt as though I had given birth to a new baby.

Life in Washington in the early 1900s was a new and delightful experience. Most of us young fellows were getting only $1,000 to $1,200 a year, but as we were traveling with expenses paid for nine months of the year, we spent little money in the field, and like the lumberjack in from the woods, we could blow most of twelve months' salary in three months, so we were fairly rich. Of course, a dollar was a dollar in those days when a drink in a good bar was priced at two for a quarter, and good theater seats $1.50. We went to the theater nearly every week and did a little innocent roistering, besides working hard through the office day.

Sometimes some of us would have what we called a millionaire dinner. We would put on evening clothes and go to one of the best places—the Shoreham or the Willard or the Raleigh. In those days there was much more ceremony and formality about a good restaurant dinner. The waiter would bring a big steak *au Béarnaise*, or something of the sort, bordered with mushrooms and green peas and little carrots, in a covered silver dish, and bow and open the dish for inspection. "Shall I serve it, sir?" Then with a very sharp knife, he would cut off the delicious pink slices and serve our plate and our wine with just the right degree of deference.

I think the art of really dining ceremoniously has disappeared—or perhaps it is only youth that has gone.

The next season, 1904, was a repetition of the previous year. The boundary crew was again dispersed to ride the western mountains and forests. This time I worked in Montana and Wyoming, and covered the Gallatin, my home country that I had ridden many times as a boy, parts of what is now the Lewis and Clark National Forest, and reexamined the boundaries of the Bighorn in Wyoming, which I covered in company with Lew Barrett of the General Land Office. I polished a lot of leather that year and had many adventures by field and stream. In the late fall I again returned to Washington to work up maps and reports.

The spring of 1905 saw a new chapter opening for the Forest Service. Gifford Pinchot had finally persuaded the administration that the forest reserves should be transferred from the General Land Office in the Department of Interior to the Department of Agriculture, and management placed under the Forest Service. Now we had a real job of forest management on our hands. The Forest Service took over from the Land Office all the forest reserve personnel, good, bad, and indifferent. The immediate job was one of inspection to weed out the incompetent political employees, replace them with new men, and at the same time to organize all the new national forests recently created by presidential proclamation and not yet under administration. It was like a fresh wind blowing through an old, corrupt, and hide-bound organization. We went to it with the enthusiasm of youth. A lot of us young fellows in our twenties, with the vast experience of two years on the Boundary Survey, were pitchforked by G.P. into jobs as general inspectors and sent west to see what we could find out. Being a native of Montana I was greatly pleased when G.P. called me in and told me that my inspection field would be Montana and Wyoming.

I have recently run across some of my old inspection reports in the closed files, and speaking perhaps without due modesty, I am really surprised how good and comprehensive they were. Perhaps our youth made us bold and self-confident, but also the knowledge that aside from G.P. himself and Overton Price, his assistant, we had about as much experience as anybody else, although under present standards our experience would not qualify us for a job as district ranger.[15]

A new ranger and supervisor personnel was the first problem—to fill in the new forests, and replace the incompetents weeded out from the GLO personnel we had inherited. G.P. promised the western people that so far as possible the reserves would be put in charge of local men who knew the country and its traditions. As pioneer conditions prevailed, the aim was to select competent woodsmen for rangers—men who could shoot straight, handle horses, travel with a pack outfit in the hills, and generally take care of themselves outdoors.

In contrast to the present-day purely written civil service examination, the original tests included two days of field events and one day for the written portion. The field test included rifle and pistol shooting at a target, riding a horse, putting on a pack, a simple exercise in compass surveying and pacing, the use of an axe, and cruising of a block of timber.

I conducted four such examinations in 1905, in Montana, at Missoula, Bozeman, Virginia City, and Neihart. From twenty to thirty men turned out at each place of examination. They included all sorts from barbers and barkeeps to first-class woodsmen or cowpunchers. We usually proceeded first to the local target range for the rifle and pistol shooting, which aroused great interest and competition. My old friend Walt Derrick tells with great glee how his first pistol bullet hit a rock thirty feet in front of him and ricocheted to the target to become firmly embedded in the bull's-eye. He claims I allowed him the bull's-eye since the bullet was there to establish it.

Most of the men got by fairly well with the horseback riding since everybody rode a horse in those days, but from the way a man approached a horse and mounted it was not hard to tell the good horsemen.

The packing was the most fun. Obviously some of the men had never put on a pack before, and they were required to cargo up a miscellaneous outfit of camp equipment and grub, and pack it properly without the use of alforjas.[16] Many and curious were the hitches used. I remember one fellow at Neihart[17] who, after precariously balancing the two packs on the saddle, took the lash rope and wound it full length around the horse and over the pack. I asked him what he called the hitch, and he said it was the "Oregon Wind."

The second day everybody mounted horses or buggies and we proceeded to the nearest timber for the axe and cruising work. I usually picked a tough Douglas-fir for each man's chopping demonstration. Some of them, of course, put the tree down in a workmanlike manner. Others went at it like some of our green CCC boys. I recall one barber who, after painfully beavering around his tree for ten minutes, stopped to wipe his steaming brow. One of the boys called to him, "Joe, it's about time for you to stop and hone your razor."

After the timber cruising, which finished the field test, we generally had a horse race back to town. I specially remember the race at Bozeman . . . . We came down Sourdough Canyon hell for leather, and nobody succeeded in passing me in the ten miles to Bozeman. These examinations were really effective. The written test eliminated the illiterates, and the field tests insured that we got experienced hands. We got a lot of good men from these examinations, some of whom later rose to places of importance in the Forest Service.

My first real inspection job was the Gallatin, in my own home country. At that time it was only a small unit—four or five townships—which had been reserved some years previously to cover some of the important watersheds of the Gallatin Valley. Mike Langohr, the supervisor, was the sole forest officer.[18] Mike wasn't so bad at that, but there really wasn't much to do in this small area, or at least he couldn't see what there was to do, and he shouldn't be blamed for also running a greenhouse and florist shop on the side; the Land Office had never objected. However, after my inspection report, Mike had to choose between the supervisorship and the greenhouse, and he chose to resign with no hard feelings.

I was able to make headquarters in my father's home in Bozeman, which was very pleasant for me, and between field jobs laboriously pecked out my reports on a little Blickensderfer portable typewriter.

My next assignment was a general inspection of the Lewis and Clark South, a vast area of wilderness country on the Blackfoot, Swan, Flathead, and Sun Rivers, and it was truly a wilderness at that time—in fact it is still one of the largest and finest wilderness areas left in the United States.[19]

Headquarters in 1905 were in Ovando, a small town sixty miles north of Missoula. The previous supervisor had been Gus Moser, and many tales are told of his performance. It is alleged that he and his wife used to meet rangers coming in for their monthly paychecks and mail, and that her wiles and other attractions, together with Gus's superior skill at poker, usually resulted in separating the rangers from most of their pay.

Moser was succeeded by Bliss, who was supervisor at the time of my inspection. He was a nice old man, but quite incompetent, and his only excursions to the forest were drives in a buckboard over the only road in the reserve, to Holland Lake at the head of the Swan River. Fortunately for him, he had an excellent and vigorous head ranger in Page Bunker. Bunker and I outfitted in Ovando, with one packhorse and a saddle horse apiece. For a four week's trip, of necessity we traveled light, with only essential basic foods. We took no canned goods, and we both agreed that potatoes were an unnecessary weight when one could get the same nourishment from rice at one-tenth the weight. We rode up the North Fork of the Blackfoot, across the range to the Dearborn, and north along the east side of the mountains. Then we struck up the Teton, and down the North Fork of the Sun River. We undertook to cross the main range just south of the Chinese Wall to White River, but ran into an early fall snowstorm, which drove us back.[20] I recall that day's ride as the time I had the best meal I ever had in my life.

At about four in the afternoon we were riding down the Sun River through six inches of fresh snow, cold, wet, and hungry. As we rode into Pretty Prairie, here was an old trapper, Eb Dickens, camped beside the trail. He wasted no time in salutations. "Get down and eat" were his first words. We dismounted stiffly and went to his fire. Eb had a big pot of coffee on the coals, and a Dutch oven full of the most delicious elk stew, big chunks of prime elk meat cooked till they were really tender, and plenty of potatoes, carrots, and onions blended into a fragrant mulligan. We tied into it properly, and it is a feed that has remained in my memory ever since.

As we could not get through to White River we returned to Ovando via the Dearborn. It is interesting that we saw no big game on that month's trip, though we ate grouse nearly every day, knocking their heads off with our .30-.30 rifles. From unrestricted hunting and no game laws the big game population of Montana probably reached its low point in the early 1900s. In that same country today, several hundred elk are killed every fall, and the sight of elk, goats, and deer is common.

Action in Washington was prompt on receipt of my inspection report. Bliss was removed and Bunker made supervisor. I do not know how such quick action was possible under civil service regulations. At the present time it would require months of correspondence and hearings, and a stack of documents a foot high. Perhaps we were fortunate that the civil service was still in its infancy, and had not yet built up too many regulations. We needed expedition to clean house, and we got it.

I was due for a surprise on my next inspection job—the Lewis and Clark North. That included at that time all the country now in Glacier National Park, and the country northwest of Kalispell in the Whitefish Range. I knew that F. N. Haines, the supervisor, was a political appointee from the Middle West, and fully expected to find another Bliss or worse.[21] Mr. Haines told me how he came to be appointed. He had been active in Republican politics in his hometown in Indiana, and one day one of the senators from his state called him in and said, "Mr. Haines, I have two positions at my disposal. One is a postmastership; the other a supervisor in Montana. You can have either one." Haines said he did not know a spruce tree from a pine, but he wanted to go west, so he chose the supervisorship. Actually, in spite of his background, he made a good supervisor for the times. There was little or no timber business yet, and he did not need to be a forester. The main job was opening up a wilderness, and Haines turned out to be an enthusiastic hunter, and did a lot of good work building trails, bridges, and ranger stations. He had some mighty good men as rangers. I especially remember old "Death on the Trail" Reynolds,[22] Frank Liebig,[23] and Fred Herrig, one of Roosevelt's old ranch hands.[24]

On the whole, the rangers inherited from the Land Office organization were much better than their supervisors. The salary was small enough, about $900 a year and furnish your own horses and grub, so that the job was not much of a political plum, and while some were useless loafers and had to be weeded out, there was a good backbone of fine men who loved the mountain country and stayed with the low-paid job because it fitted them. Such men we gladly retained.

One of my most arduous inspection jobs was in January 1906. For some unknown reason the Washington office wired me to make an inspection of the Highwood Mountain Reserve at once.[25] A field trip to the Highwoods in January is no picnic. It is one of the coldest regions in the United States. I drove out from Fort Benton thirty miles or so across the open plains to Highwood in an open bobsleigh, with the thermometer 30°F or more below zero, and the wind right off the North Pole. A man named Thain was supervisor, and we took saddle horses and rode the reserve, stopping at ranches.[26] It was a poor time to see the condition of the range, but at any rate I got acquainted with some of the ranchers and got their reaction to the administration, which was generally favorable. I don't think it got above thirty degrees below zero on the whole trip, and if the Washington office merely wanted to know how tough I was, I certainly demonstrated.

After that winter trip I was not sorry to receive instructions to go in for a detail in the Washington office. I spent three or four months there getting my first experience in administration from the Washington end.

At that time the western forests were divided into three administrative districts: the northern Rockies, the southern Rockies, and the Pacific coast. A sort of chief of operations was responsible for each, handling personnel, allotments, and improvements. I had the northern district, Smith Riley the southern, and Coert DuBois the Pacific coast. These positions were rotated as inspectors came in from the field.

Gifford Pinchot was a hard taskmaster for us young fellows. We had a buzzer for interoffice signals, but G.P. had a special buzzer of his own for our quarters, one buzz for me, two for Riley, and three for DuBois—and this buzzer had a tone like a rattlesnake that fairly lifted one out of his chair and across the room when G.P. pressed it. When we wrote a letter for G.P. to sign we always awaited in fear and trembling. If he signed it without change, it was an occasion of triumph. Often the letter came back with a big blue question mark scrawled across it. Then we had to figure out if it was basically wrong or merely a punctuation point out of place. G.P. was merciless with careless errors. I recall one reply I prepared for a senator asking for the total area of national forests. The stenographer got an extra zero in my figure, which I failed to detect, and G.P. gave me a panning for carelessness which I will never forget. It was a hard school, but good training for us, and the surprising thing is that we never lost our devotion and high regard for G.P.

He was a man of the most impressive appearance and magnetic personality. It was his almost religious devotion to the cause of forestry and conservation that inspired a loyalty and interest in the job for its own sake that was probably never equaled in any government bureau. In some ways his character resembled that of Franklin D. Roosevelt. Both men professed, and I think sincerely, the greatest solicitude for the small man—the underdog. At the same time, both were aristocrats by birth, training, environment, and inherited wealth. While G.P. could be very affable and free and easy with woodsmen and mountain men and small ranchers, he never could make himself one of them; similar to Roosevelt, he was always the aristocrat, and his affability contained something of patronage. One never forgot that he was Gifford Pinchot, the chief, and no one never dreamed of taking any liberties with him. I recall one young man in the office routing a document to his desk marked simply "Pinchot." He was given a severe reprimand for leaving off the "Mr."

Once a month the members of the newly organized Society of American Foresters used to go to his house on Rhode Island Avenue for a society meeting in his baronial library, followed invariably by refreshments of baked apples and cream.[27] Sometimes he took some of us down into his basement for pistol shooting at a target. There were few of us who could equal him at the game.

Salaries in the early Forest Service were very low. They ran from $1,500 to $2,000 for forest supervisors, and $900 to $1,400 for rangers. Inspectors got $1,500 to $1,700. G.P.'s own pay was $3,600 a year. Of course since he had abundant personal means his own salary meant very little to

FIG. 13. Elers Koch in Washington DC, 1906.

him, and he made no effort to have it raised, but being the top position it kept all other salaries down to a low level. I doubt if he ever realized the difficulties of a man with a family living on such a low income.

Washington bureaucracy in the early 1900s was at its height for formality, red tape, and delay in action. I had seen something of the Land Office forestry division, and it was typical of the worst of what we think by the term "bureaucracy." A case coming in for action—for instance an application for a ditch right-of-way or a timber sale, and all such cases then had to come to Washington—was examined by a clerk, given a case number, wrapped in a blue paper jacket, and what was called "docketed," placed in the files at the back of a similar lot of cases. The phrase "handled in due course" was exactly descriptive of subsequent action. It never seemed to occur to these leisurely employees that action on a simple application might be taken the same day or the same week as received, or that it was really no more work to keep action current than always three months behind. When the transfer of the forest reserves was made to the Forest Service, most of the old leisurely departmental methods were swept out, and good business management adopted. When I first came to Washington, the greatest degree of formality, particularly between departments, prevailed. For instance, the standard form prescribed for preparing a letter from the secretary of agriculture to the secretary of interior called for a salutation, "The Honorable, The Secretary of Interior, Sir," and ended with "I have the honor to be, Sir, very respectfully, Your Obedient Servant, Secretary of Agriculture." G.P. was probably the first bureau chief to provide for commencing letters, "Dear Mr. Blank," and ending with "Very truly yours." He was insistent on letters being human, and couched in plain straightforward English, with no departmental gobbledygook, a word that at that time had not been invented.

I often think what a wonderful thing it was to have a government bureau with nothing but young men in it. There was no retirement law at that time, and most of the other bureaus were more or less bogged down with superannuated old men and women. There was one Land Office section where we had to go occasionally to obtain information on the status of public lands. We used to call it "The Hall of the Ancients,"—a great hall full of desks, all occupied by grey-bearded men and grey-haired women laboriously copying records by hand.

In the new Forest Service, G.P. himself, and his top assistants, Price, [George] Woodruff, and Potter, were all in their late thirties or early forties.[28] Most of the rest of us were still in our twenties and chiefly unmarried. There was no inheritance of departmental methods or red tape inhibition in our cosmos. It was largely this youth and freshness of view that caused the Forest Service to become generally recognized as one of the most efficient of government offices. I often think that if the old men in control of the governments of the world could be suddenly and painlessly eliminated, and affairs turned over to young men under forty, we might get somewhere.

The Forest Service is now forty-two years older than it was in 1906; the young men of that day are now old men, and of course, the average age of the whole service is much higher. In my latest visits to the Washington office I have felt that the dry rot of departmentalism is slowly creeping even into the younger services. Governmental procedure tends to get more and more complicated though much of this is forced on the bureaus by congressional acts, requirements of the General Accounting Office, and the civil service. Certainly it takes three to four times more clerks to handle a given activity than it did in the early days of the Forest Service.

My detail in Washington over, I was back in the field again in the spring of 1906 making another round of inspections, and helping to get the new national forests organized. Most of the supervisors were new, either by promotion from ranger positions, or by appointment from the new civil service eligible list. It was the job of the inspector to encourage the new men, help them get oriented in their jobs, and give them helpful advice on their problems. Most of them responded well to this, and we were gradually building up a fine force of men. Occasionally we had the disagreeable job of recommending dismissal of incompetents or misfits.

One of the forests I inspected during the summer was the Madison.[29] The supervisor was Jasper B. Seeley, who had been one of the old-time rangers under the Land Office, and had worked under Gus Moser on the Lewis and Clark.[30] Seeley was a hard and tough man with a good

FIG. 14. (*top*) Gerda Koch at home at 420 E. Beckwith Avenue in Missoula, Montana, circa 1908. (*bottom*) Elers and Gerda Koch and their three sons (*left to right:* Peter, Thomas, and Stanley). (*opposite*) Exterior of Koch family home on Beckwith Avenue.

sense of justice, but inclined to enforce regulations up to the hilt, and a good many complaints had been coming in to Washington. He told me one characteristic story. While he was working as ranger under Gus Moser, he caught a man setting a forest fire, arrested him, and brought him to Ovando to the supervisor. Moser, for some reason, was unwilling to bring the case to trial, and after waiting two or three days, Seeley, in disgust at the lack of action, started to return to headquarters with his prisoner. Halfway there, Seeley decided that if the law would not act he would see that justice was done himself. He stopped the horses, jerked the man off his saddle, and proceeded to half flay him with a blacksnake whip he carried.

I made a three-week trip over the forest with Seeley with a team and a buckboard, stopping chiefly at ranches, where I had a chance to talk to the local people. There was some hostility to the Forest Service, but on the whole the people were friendly except in the mining region around Virginia City. Seeley had been very strict in enforcing regulations regarding timber cutting for mining purposes, and the miners generally did not like it. When my inspection report went in, G.P. sent Seeley a typical letter. Illustrating his point, he said, "If you are out on the forest and come across a man who has broken his wagon tongue and cut a sapling to fix it, don't prosecute him for timber trespass, but get off your horse and help him fix it." Seeley served many years thereafter, and made a first-rate supervisor.

In the winter of 1906 and 1907 all the general inspectors who had been making headquarters in Washington were moved permanently to the West. Six inspection districts were set up, which were the forerunners of the regional offices to be established a couple of years later. I could have remained an inspector, but I had been knocking all around the West for four years. I wanted to get married, and concluded that being a forest supervisor with definite responsibility for a particular tract of forest was the most attractive and soul-satisfying job in the service. G.P. encouraged me in the idea, since he had promised that the national forests would be in charge of western men, and I was one of the few western men who was also a forest school graduate.

In December 1906, I moved to Missoula with all my lares and penates, including a new bride [Gerda],[31] and took over administration of the Lolo, Bitterroot, and Missoula National Forests.[32]

CHAPTER 3

Forest Supervisor: 1907–1918

I now had just what I wanted. There is no other job on earth quite equal to that of a forest supervisor. He controls an estate of a million or two million acres of forest and mountain land, on which he is given a free hand to administer, develop, protect, and best of all, to watch its growth and improvement from year to year. The feeling of proprietorship of a good supervisor is so great that it is almost as though he owned the land himself, and he gets about the same pleasure and satisfaction out of it.

I started temporarily with about two million acres, the Montana division of the Bitterroot Forest, which had already been several years under administration, the newly created Lolo Forest west of Missoula, a portion of the new Hellgate Forest east of the Bitterroot Valley, and the new Missoula Forest north of Missoula—all of it practically unknown to me, and much of it unmapped and unexplored.[1]

There was everything to do: the selection and appointment of an adequate ranger force, the exploration and mapping of the vast territory, ranger stations to locate and build, the planning, location, and construction of a trail system, and later a telephone system—we had not yet

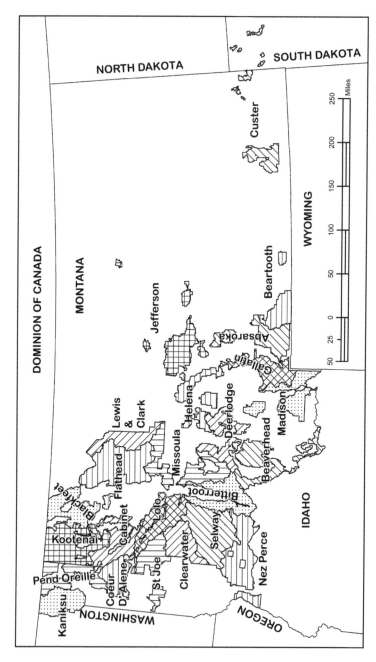

FIG. 15. National forests as they existed in 1913 in District One. Courtesy of Northern Region, USDA Forest Service.

reached the stage of thinking about road building. There were numerous timber trespasses to locate and settle, and land claims to examine and adjudicate. Then of course when summer came on, there was the ever present problem of forest fires.

I established an office in a couple of rooms in the old Hammond Building, and installed an ancient Oliver typewriter and a few filing cases.[2] At first I picked out my own letters with two fingers, but soon acquired a clerk.

In the field I immediately had to learn two new tricks—to use web snowshoes, and to carry a pack on my back. I had used skis some as a boy in Bozeman, but never snowshoes. I had never worked in deep snow country, and was amazed at how snow piled up in the west end of the Lolo Forest—six, eight, or ten feet, even fifteen or twenty on the high divides. There was no getting off the railroad track in winter without snowshoes, and I quickly picked up the art.

As to backpacking, I had come from a horse country, and the idea of a man carrying a pack on his back was practically new to me. Here in western Montana at that time everybody carried his own bedroll, and as horses were not abundant we had to learn to take a forty- or fifty-pound pack to do any exploring, particularly in winter. I never did like to carry a backpack; it takes all the joy out of life. I am not very big or physically strong, but eventually learned through necessity to handle a pack along with the rest.

One of the first jobs was to build up a ranger personnel. I had inherited from the old Bitterroot five or six rangers. One of these, Than Wilkerson, who had come into the service almost from the beginning, was a top man, and I owe much to him. A couple of the others, political appointees under the Land Office, I had to get rid of the first year. Two men I had during the first year were towers of strength to me. There was John D. Jones, a recent graduate from the University of Montana, a rangy tireless fellow, brought up in western Montana. I gave him a free hand on the new Lolo Forest to see what he could find out, locate timber trespass, check out fraudulent claims, make some timber sales where needed, and generally find out what was going on. He covered a tremendous amount of territory in the first year, and continually sent in good information. The other man, my assistant supervisor, Wilford W. White, I count as one of my oldest friends.[3] He was a recent graduate in forestry from Cornell, and I put him largely on timber work, cruising and looking after sale of timber.

I generally, through the next year or so, picked up a number of good men as rangers. Old Frank Hahn, one of the old-time rangers under the Land Office, was one of the best. He was a man of not much education, but an excellent woodsman, and as honest, reliable, and loyal as the day is long. I have made many a hard trip with Frank Hahn, and one could always be sure of his good humor, courage, and common sense. In spite of his lack of education, he was a splendid organizer, and could throw out and man a string of fire camps faster than any man I knew. I got most of my early lessons in fire fighting from him.

Another ranger, Rochester I will call him though that is not his name, will always stand out in my memory as one of the strangest and most bizarre characters I have ever met. He was an expert mechanic, capable of earning a high wage at his trade, but through some quirk of his nature he had given up his job and had taken a remote and desolate homestead back in the timber, accessible only by pack trail, where he lived with his wife, two daughters, and a small son. He came down and took the ranger examination, and I was impressed by his intelligence, ability, and fine appearance. He did much good and efficient work for me for several years, but I always had a feeling of something strange and sinister about him. He reminded me of Dark Bidwell, one of Vardis Fisher's characters.[4] He had a streak of cold cruelty in him which sometimes cropped out. I have seen him deliberately beat a tired and refractory horse with a wire whip, not in a passion, but with a cold and repressed deliberation.

A few years after he was appointed ranger, a terrible tragedy occurred. He was then staying at the old St. Regis ranger station, a rather remote place, accessible only by rail or a speeder from the N. P. [Northern Pacific] railroad track. At the time his wife and daughter were away, and he was alone in the cabin with his little son, about five years old. There was a neighboring homesteader, whose house was about two hundred yards from the ranger station, who had two great black-and-white dogs of some mixed breed. One winter day the little boy started to go over to his neighbor, scuffling happily along through a newly fallen snow. Halfway over there, the two savage dogs fell on him, knocked him down, and in full sight of his father, tore his throat wide open. Rochester reached over the door for his rifle and shot both dogs, but it was too late to save the boy's life.

After that terrible episode he was more morose and reserved than usual, but I hardly expected the next development. I came home from the office one day and found my wife very much upset. Mrs. Rochester and her two daughters had been in to see her, and told a most horrifying tale of incest carried on over several years. They had left Rochester, and were in a panic as to what he might do. I called up Rochester on the phone and told him I wanted to see him right away. He came in on a late train, and I met him alone in my office about eleven o'clock at night. I could see by the bulge on his hip that he had a gun on him, and I confess I was not too comfortable about confronting him. I told him straight out that I knew what had been going on, and there was no place in the service for him. I shoved a resignation blank across the desk, "Sign that." He gave me a cold stare, picked up the pen and signed, and strode out of the office. He was later tried in county court for incest, but was acquitted, though I never had any doubt about his guilt after the story that Mrs. Rochester and the girls told my wife. Doubtless the man was mentally unbalanced at times.

Personnel cases are common in a large organization. Over a period of several years, in the process of getting an efficient ranger force organized, I have had to get rid of six or eight men for various reasons. Every one of these cases was settled quietly and promptly by presenting my case and permitting the man to sign a resignation blank, and I feel sure that in no case was any injustice perpetrated.

Such a procedure in government service nowadays would be anathema. It is now a difficult and serious matter to get rid of an inefficient civil service employee, and it is rarely done without piling up several inches of documents, after the case has been considered by the supervisor, the regional forester, the Department of Agriculture, and finally the Civil Service Commission. Perhaps all this is necessary for protection of employees, though I think it is overdone, but it is fortunate that in the formative years of the Forest Service things could be done with more dispatch.

The first spring after arriving in Missoula, Gerda and I went over to Bozeman to get my horses. My cousin Richard Biering had given us the splendid wedding present of a pair of three-quarter Hambletonian bay horses, broke both to harness and saddle. Pointer was really a fine horse. I used him most of the time as my saddle horse, and several times rode him up to sixty miles in a day. He was full of life, and yet a good reliable horse on mountain trails. The other horse, Blitzen, was a coarser animal, but a good strong beast, and they made a good team.

We drove over from Bozeman to Missoula in a light buggy, 240 miles, which took five and a half days. Now one drives it in a car in five and a half hours. That is a good measure of the change in transportation in forty-five years. One long day's travel then is closely equivalent to one hour in a car. It was sheer pleasure jogging over the hilly dirt road with the team, and we easily made about forty miles a day, stopping at the smaller towns, though one night we enjoyed the luxury of the Thornton Hotel in Butte.

I bought a light, strong spring wagon for field trips, and a buckskin pony for Gerda. Buck was a nice little horse with only one bad fault—it was almost impossible to catch him outside a corral, and he had the most devilish ability to avoid being driven in from pasture. The rangers got so they hated to have him left in their pastures, as he usually led the whole bunch in a break back.

In the first few years of my supervisorship, I used frequently to take Gerda along on the easier field trips. The spring wagon would be loaded with camp outfit, beds and saddles, and with little Buck trotting behind the rig we were ready at any time to transfer from wheels to a pack outfit when I wanted to leave the road. Wherever the little nine-by-nine teepee tent was pitched with a fire in front of it was home. Those first years of exploration, inspection, and administration of my new domain were among the best years of my life.

FIG. 16. (*top*) Gerda Koch in the field. (*bottom*) Gerda driving the spring wagon with a pair of three-quarter Hambeltonians.

My first large sale of timber was in the Bitterroot. The Anaconda Copper Mining Company owned large timber tracts in the valley, and since they were logging up to the border of one of the best units of ponderosa pine on the forest, they applied to buy the timber. It was duly advertised, and no one expected any competition, but unexpectedly an Idaho outfit, Hitt and Melquist, stepped in and bid $4.03 a thousand for the timber. The Anaconda Company had practically a monopoly on the timber business in the Bitterroot, and objected strongly to seeing a new competitive outfit come into the picture. They finally made a deal with Hitt and Melquist, and took the contract over at a considerable profit to the original bidder.

This was my first opportunity to really apply the principles of forestry I had learned at Yale. I knew all about the different silvicultural systems in theory, the shelterwood system, the selection system, the single seed tree system, and so on, as used in Europe, but when it came to apply them in our native timber with no precedent to go on, that was something else. I got a crew of rangers together and we started marking the timber to be cut. Fortunately, ponderosa pine, or yellow pine as it was commonly called, lends itself well to commonsense forestry. One approaches a great yellow-bark pine with the crown beginning to thin out and flatten at the top. No doubt about that fellow; he is mature and ready to cut, and the sharp marking axe takes a chip from the bark, and the raised letters *US* on the poll of the axe stamp him for removal. Perhaps the next tree is a black-barked tree with a full crown. That fellow is growing fast and we will leave him for the next cut. So one goes through the stand, taking out the mature trees and leaving the more thrifty to grow. This is the best part of a forester's work; now we are practicing real forestry.

Shortly after we had started the marking job, we had an inspection visit from Gifford Pinchot, who approved of most of what we had done, but felt we had been cutting too heavily, and made us go back and mark out some of the blazes on doubtful trees with red paint. I have been back to this first timber sale many times in subsequent years. After forty-five years it is a pleasure to see the results. The trees have grown enough so that the area is ready for a second cut, and all the openings have seeded up densely to a fine new crop of sapling pine and fir.

We had a good deal of trouble with the company enforcing the terms of the contract, since it was their first experience in buying national forest timber. Actually the requirements were not burdensome. It is true that we were not clear-cutting, as the company was accustomed to doing on its own lands, and many good merchantable trees were left to grow, but it resulted in their getting a bigger and better run of logs. They particularly objected to piling and burning the slash; nobody had ever heard of such foolishness. The lumber industry is probably the most conservative manufacturing industry in the world—at least it was at that time, although the adoption of modern machine methods has begun to get them out of the rut of old-time logging traditions handed down from Maine to the Lake States, and from the Lake States to the Northwest.[5]

Money for operating expenses was always tight in the early days of the Forest Service. I had a bare allowance for salaries, office rental, and a small amount for travel and incidentals. In the summer of 1907, I got the first allotments for trail and telephone construction, and something for ranger stations. We built the first Forest Service telephone line in Montana that year, about twenty miles up the West Fork of the Bitterroot. None of us knew anything about telephone construction or installation of instruments, but Than Wilkerson was equal to most any kind of a job, and the wire was strung to poles and trees in fairly good shape, and the first instrument installed after much figuring and consultation in the old ranger station at Alta.[6] I shall never forget the thrill of talking through from that remote spot by long distance to Missoula. The idea that we woodsmen could put in twenty miles of telephone that really worked! There is now a network of telephone lines all over the national forests, and telephoning is commonplace, but I still feel a bit overcome by the magic of talking from the wilderness to the outside by our own handiwork. Even radio communication is now becoming so commonplace that perhaps sometime most of our telephone lines through the hills will be abandoned.

Trail construction was always my favorite undertaking. I tried to locate most of our trail routes personally before construction started, and when one has spent many arduous hours painfully toiling up a steep timbered creek bottom, obstructed by brush, rocks, swamp, and down timber, and a few months later rides a horse easily up a cleared and graded trail—that is a real satisfaction; that is opening up the wilderness. For my first major trail project I decided to build a trail along the summit of the main Bitterroot Range, which forms the divide between Montana and Idaho. I put out three trail crews in the late summer, but did not get to inspect them until late October. It was perfect bright blue fall weather, with the tamaracks and cottonwoods shining golden in the sun when I met Ranger Watson at Lolo Pass with his saddle and packhorse and our bedrolls and provisions for a few days. We had thirty miles of high divide to ride before we would hit the first section of the new trail, our only guide being the monuments set by the State Line Boundary Survey. In spite of the rough going, the first day was pure joy, riding the high divide in glorious weather, with the whole world of endless peaks and ridges on either side. Riding such a high divide, I never swing onto my horse in the morning without Kipling's lines from "Screw Guns" running through my head:

> Smokin' my pipe in the mountings, sniffin' the morning cool,
> I walks in my old brown gaiters long o' my old brown mule.
> The eagles is screamin' around us, the river's a-moanin' below,
> We're clear o' the pine an' the oak-scrub, we're out on the rocks
>   an' the snow.

The second day we made the serious error of getting off on a spur ridge which seemed higher than the main divide. We discovered our mistake when we had gone about two miles by the absence of the state line monuments, and looking across the head of a creek on the Idaho side I could see with my field glasses a monument on a distant ridge. Reluctant to retrace our steps, we foolishly decided to cut straight down across the creek and back up to the main divide. We got into the worst country I ever took a horse through, thick alder brush over broken rock, down timber, steep slopes, and every obstacle the mountains can offer to a horseman. We half killed the horses, forcing them over rocks and jumping down timber. We jumped them over anything we could get the bridles over, but many times we had a horse down between the logs and the rocks. After we got into that mess we could not retreat, and had to force our way through it. By the time we got back on the divide the animals were in pretty bad shape, and poor Pointer had lost two shoes in the rocks and was limping badly.

We proceeded more cautiously, but it was the end of the fifth day when we reached Fish Lake, which we had expected to attain in two days. In camp that night we shook the last flour from the sack and ate the last bacon and potatoes. One of the trail crews had started from here west, and we figured by following this new trail we would be in their camp by night. We rode cheerfully along the new trail, and in midafternoon reached the end of the trail, and the trail camp, deserted. Apparently the late September snowstorm had driven the crew out of the mountains. Here we were—fifty miles back in the hills, and nothing to eat. There was nothing for it but to turn back to Fish Lake. We searched the camp for anything in the way of food, and on the garbage dump we found two boiled potatoes and a strip of bacon rind. With these trophies we retraced our way to Fish Lake, which we reached about dark. We decided to push on down Fish Creek, where a trail led to the settlements. The trail plunged immediately into a dense cedar forest, so black I could hardly see my horse's ears. I let Pointer have his head, and somehow we managed to stay on the trail for the most part. Two hours of this was enough, and we dismounted, unpacked, and tied up the tired animals, while we heated up the two boiled potatoes with grease from the bacon rind. We made it out to the railroad late the next day, but by the time I got Pointer back to Missoula he was not much good for the rest of that fall.

I had to have some place for my rangers to live, and for the first few years one of the chief activities was location and surveying of suitable ranger station sites, and putting up buildings and pasture fences. The houses were for the most part rather primitive log structures with shake roofs, largely built by ranger labor. Real money for materials was so scarce that every cent had to be conserved. One way or another we got most of the rangers housed, though I find that in the course of years most of my old ranger stations have been abandoned. Even now I can hardly realize what a complete change in organization and methods has been effected by roads and automobiles, contrasted with a horse economy. The number of ranger districts has been greatly reduced, and the rangers are now being settled in town or just outside of towns, with good modern houses equipped with central heating, excellent plumbing, and electric ranges. Quite a contrast to our first ranger stations, but we were proud of them, and they served the pioneer purposes.

The establishment of the forest reserves, or national forests, as they were now called, came as a surprise and shock to many westerners. No longer could a man homestead a valuable piece of timber, or cut timber without let or hindrance from the public domain. The stockmen particularly objected to the restrictions. They had been accustomed to free range, which anyone took who could hold it. Now to be required to get grazing permits, and even to pay grazing fees, was a hard dose for the free and independent cattle or sheep man to swallow. The bulk of the resistance to the new reserves came from the more important grazing units, particularly in Colorado and Wyoming. I never had a great deal of trouble on the Lolo and Bitterroot Forests. There was some grumbling and a few protests, but no serious adverse public reaction. Gradually most of the local people became friendly to the Forest Service. I never was much of a hand for what is commonly called public relations work. While I saw reporters from the local papers frequently and gave them the forest news, I did little in the way of propaganda. I always figured that if the Forest Service did a good job without fear or favor, opened up the country with trails, administered our timber sales and grazing permits fairly, kept down the forest fires, and made a good showing in efficiency and economy, the works would speak for themselves, and much education and propaganda were unnecessary. I never had any serious complaints or appeal cases in my twelve years as supervisor.

The years 1907 and 1908 were particularly active ones in the Lolo Forest. The Milwaukee Railroad was just building. It crossed considerable government land, and there was much business connected with rights-of-way, permits for contractor's buildings, timber sales, and all the other activities connected with a big railroad job. Of course there was fire strung along the whole length of the line in the process of clearing the right-of-way. Fortunately 1907 was a wet year, and we managed to hold things in check with little loss. I got my first baptism in large-scale fire fighting that summer, and learned a great deal that was useful later on.

The biggest job on the railroad was construction of the St. Paul Pass tunnel under the Bitterroot Range.[7] Work went on winter and summer, in spite of a terrific snowfall often of ten or twelve feet which nearly buried operations. Construction towns sprang up on each side of the pass—Grand Forks in Idaho and Taft in Montana. Taft became the only real example of a tough frontier town such as the western story writers feature that I have come across in all my western experience. It was really a wide-open town, though more sordid than picturesque. The hard-rock tunnel miners, largely Slavic, had to have their recreation, which was drink, women, and gambling, and Taft furnished it plentifully. I avoided the place as much as I could, but had to spend an occasional night there, but not to sleep. The roistering went on day and night, with three tunnel shifts working.

There were two major places which were combination saloons, gambling dens, and dance halls, besides a long row of cribs on one end of the street. The bars were lined with hard-faced dance hall girls, ready to separate the hard-rock miners from their wages, and every kind of gambling game going wide open.

I recall spending one night there with one of the rangers. After trying vainly to sleep in our room above one of the bars, we decided to go down and look the place over, and drifted through both the big joints. The gambling games were, of course, all crooked, and did not tempt me much, but I idly dropped a few quarters in one of the slot machines. In those days slot machines produced various combinations of poker hands on card faces, rather than the plums, pears, and cherries which are today for some reason considered less wicked. To my surprise I happened to hit the jackpot, and the machine disgorged a double handful of quarters, which overran the cup and spilled on the floor. It seemed to me that every girl in the place made a grab for me. One big blonde in a very low-cut dress had her arm tightly around my neck. I didn't mind setting up a few drinks, but those girls were a little much for my Presbyterian upbringing, and I ducked under the arm of the blond and escaped through the door, stuffing quarters in every pocket—an inglorious exit. The tale is generally told that when the big snow went off in the spring of 1908, five or six dead bodies were exposed at the rear doors of the two dance halls.

My neighbor, Supervisor Roscoe Haines, over on the Idaho side of the line, also had his troubles with the construction job.[8] The story is that he sent a telegram to the district office in Missoula, "Two undesirable prostitutes established on government land. What should I do?" The wire fell into the hands of old Major F. A. Fenn for action. The major, an old-timer from Kooskia, Idaho, with a keen sense of humor, wired back, "Better get two desirable ones."

At that time Idaho was officially dry, and Montana very wet. Since there was much demand for wet goods at Grand Forks in Idaho, there was a constant flow of smuggled liquor over the line from Taft. One time, Ranger Frank Hahn and I were cruising through the timber at the top of the divide which formed the state line, and ran into an amazing cache set down in a heap in the timber with apparently no one on guard. There were cases and cases of Scotch, bourbon, and rye, champagne and other wines, brandy and rum, enough to stock a good-sized saloon. We stopped and looked at it a minute and I said to Frank, "I think we had better move on; we don't know anything about this." A few months later Frank told me that he had talked to a man who was hidden in the timber with his rifle trained on us. It was just as well we concealed our curiosity.

The railroad construction camp of Taft was the nearest approach in my experience to the roaring West so beloved by fiction writers. I am going to have to admit that after sixty-seven years of life in the West, and riding many thousands of miles through the range and mountain country of Montana, Wyoming, Colorado, Idaho, Washington, and California, I have never yet seen gunplay or seen a shot fired in anger. My father for some years lived a pioneer existence in the 1860s and 1870s in some of the wildest parts of Montana along the breaks of the Missouri and the

Judith Basin, his everyday associates woodhawks, wolfers, hide hunters, and Indian traders. While he may have shot with his Henry rifle a hostile Indian or two attacking his trading posts, he never carried a six-shooter, and so far as I know never owned one. As a tenderfoot direct from the University of Copenhagen, he should have been expected, in the best western story manner, to be obliged to dance at the point of a gun, but to the best of my knowledge he was always treated with the greatest of kindness and respect by his rough associates.

The truth of the matter is that the West of fiction, Hollywood, and the pulp magazines never existed. It is a most amazing dream world, gradually developed by ingenious writers, till it is almost real, with conditions and conventions so accepted that the writer steps into it with the same familiarity and assurance as if he was writing about an actual country and condition. Of course there were criminals in the West, and there were robberies and quarrels among the criminals, and shooting affairs with the peace officers. These have been exaggerated and built up until we get a picture of each cattle ranch as a feudal barony, protected only by a bunch of hired gun-packing cowboys, and every man's hand against his neighbor. There have always been criminals and shooting affairs in any part of the country, whether it be Massachusetts or Montana. It is probable that there has been more hostile lead fired in Chicago in gangster fights between themselves or with police than there ever was in the West, and yet very few citizens have ever had any personal experience or contact with such affrays, any more than the average citizen in the West in the early days.

I cannot describe our early forest rangers as picturesque characters, riding the range with a gun on each hip. They were not peace officers, but hardworking men, and while a ranger might occasionally carry a rifle or even a pistol on a trip into the backcountry in the hopes of getting a shot at a coyote, our rangers did not carry guns habitually, and certainly not when they went to town.

In the earlier days of the Forest Service rangers and supervisors furnished their own horses—at least two per man. That had its advantages, as a man naturally took good care of his own stock, and many rangers took great pride in their horses and equipment, but it was a considerable expense for a low-salaried man, even after a forage allowance was approved, and gradually most of the rangers' horses were replaced by government-owned stock. At the present time very few Forest Service officers supply their own saddle horses, and all of the pack animals in use are government owned. The Forest Service has done much to develop the art of packing, and I doubt if there is anywhere in the country as well-organized, well-equipped, and efficient pack strings or more skilled packers than the Forest Service can boast, even including the army. With the opening up of much country by roads, and the increased use in recent years of air transportation, the number of pack stock required by the Forest Service has been considerably reduced, but there is still much backcountry where transportation must be handled by pack animals over trails, and the mule will not be entirely replaced for many years.

At first we used mainly horses for pack animals, but these were gradually replaced by the more efficient mule, and in this district mules are now used almost exclusively for packing. They are more tractable than horses, much more enduring, and can carry heavier loads. The conformation of a mule's back, and his easy ambling gate, seem to fit him much better for a burden bearer than a horse. Somehow a horse always seems to resent the indignity of a pack. We had considerable difficulty in buying a sufficient supply of mules to meet our specifications, and in the early thirties a central district remount depot near Missoula was established, and the breeding of mules undertaken by the Forest Service. We now take great pride in our splendid uniform strings of pack mules. A standard string of mules is formed of seven animals, besides the packer's horse. The old-fashioned gray bell mare is no longer used; the mules learn to follow the packer's saddle horse. They are never used loose on the trail, but each mule is tied by his halter rope to a "pig tail" on the saddle of the preceding animal in the string.

The Forest Service in the Idaho and Montana region has done much to develop a perfect packsaddle and equipment. The old-fashioned sawbuck saddle was commonly used years ago, but it carried the load too high, and often lacerated the back of the unfortunate pack animal. We now use the so-called "Decker saddle" exclusively, which was developed in the mining regions of central Idaho, and somewhat modified and improved by the Forest Service. Instead of the wooden cross trees of the old sawbuck, the two side boards are connected with iron arches. Over the saddle is fastened a leather-bound canvas pad stuffed with hay or bear grass, which goes down well on each side and protects the mule from injury by the pack. This is a modification of the old-fashioned aparejo, formerly much used in the Southwest. In packing with the Decker saddle, top packs are seldom used. The load is cargoed into two side packs, each in a canvas manta securely bound with rope. Only a swing rope is used, with no lash rope and cinch. In Forest Service packing in this region the old-style diamond hitch is practically a thing of the past.

One of the jobs that seem to fall *ex officio* to forest officers is searching for lost persons in the mountains. Such cases seem to increase every year, particularly during the deer and elk hunting season, as the automobile makes it easier to get out in the hills, and all sorts of people with very slight experience in the woods think they can take their rifles and go out and get a piece of meat. Sometimes they get lost and fail to return to camp, and a call goes out for help to find them. In a surprising number of cases men with bad hearts go hunting, overexert themselves, and sit down against a tree and expire. In my day as supervisor before the general use of automobiles there were fewer inexperienced men in the woods during the hunting season, but there were always a few cases of lost men who had to be searched for.

I especially remember one instance when a couple of men from Missoula went out deer hunting in one of the canyons about twenty miles from town expecting to return the same day. They were both office men—I will call them Phillips and Roberts, though that was not their true names. Phillips was subject to Bright's disease, and had been warned not to overexert himself, and had no business on a hunting trip.[9] Neither one was much of a woodsman. They failed to return as expected, and the next morning a telephone call came in from Roberts from an outlying ranch. Phillips had gotten sick and played out, and Roberts had left him to go for help, and got lost and spent the night in a tree for fear of mountain lions. The next morning he had come out at a ranch and telephoned in to Missoula. Since they were men we knew and liked, eight or ten Forest Service men turned out for a rescue party under the leadership of W. B. Greeley, who was then regional forester.[10] We drove out to the ranch where Roberts was still staying, and found him in such an exhausted and hysterical condition that it was obvious that he could not guide us back to where he had left Phillips. He was able to describe the location in a general way, so we left him at the ranch and proceeded to the location described.

Greeley spread us out in a line within seeing distance of each other, and we proceeded to comb the area, an open stand of lodgepole pine and fir. We had not gone more than an hour when one of the men sighted something; sure enough it was our man. He was lying flat on his back, holding a pistol in his right hand across his breast, and obviously dead. Somebody had carried a couple of blankets along, and we spread one over the body and from the other made a stretcher with two straight poles. We lifted Phillips's body over to the stretcher, still covered by the blanket, and proceeded to carry him out to the nearest road, which was several miles down a steep mountain slope. There were eight of us, so with four men carrying the stretcher, we could change off every five minutes. If one has never carried a dead man it is hard to realize how heavy even a quarter of a 160-pound body becomes. When I took my turn the pole ground into my shoulder as we plunged down the steep mountain side, till it seemed as though I could not endure it another minute. We finally got to the road, loaded the body into a car, still wrapped in a blanket, and brought it to an undertaker's establishment in Missoula.

When the undertaker examined the body there was a bullet wound in the head behind the left ear. We had taken it for granted that the man died of exposure or shock, and had made no examination, though I had noticed some blood on the ear and assumed he had torn it in the brush.

Phillips's wife was ill and in a delicate condition, and Greeley, who is a pretty dominant character, took it upon himself to see that for the wife's sake the fact that Phillips had shot himself be completely hushed up. The funeral was held, and the next day Mrs. Phillips and her mother left for the East, and to this day, if she is still alive, she does not know but that her husband died a natural death. Roberts stayed in Missoula only a short time, and then threw up his job and left suddenly.

It was perhaps just as well to keep the matter secret, but I have often speculated on what actually happened. It was assumed that after Roberts left, Phillips, knowing that he would die of cold and exposure, and being terrified of the lonesomeness of the mountains, shot himself. But the gun was held in his right hand. It would take considerable unnatural contortion for a man to hold a gun in his right hand and shoot himself behind the left ear, and certainly in that case the body would sprawl out, and not lie peacefully composed with the arm across the chest. Did Roberts shoot Phillips by accident and cover it up, or perhaps did Phillips beg Roberts to shoot him before leaving him sick and dying in the woods? No one will ever know, and perhaps it is just as well.

It is surprising how seldom serious accidents befall experienced forest officers in the woods, considering the possibilities. I have often thought, in making my way alone in rough country, cruising or scouting a forest fire, perhaps through a jungle of down timber piled six or eight feet high, and jumping from log to log, "What would one do if, all alone, one fell and broke a leg?" Yet I hardly know of a case where this has happened, perhaps because most Forest Service men are properly shod with calks or sharp hobnails, and because they are trained and used to such going. The green CCC boys and some of our summer blister rust crews have many more accidents.

I remember one incident when I was out on a trip with veteran timber cruiser Jim Girard, who has a reputation as one of the best woodsmen and the toughest man in the Forest Service. We were taking a trip up Trout Creek to look over some timber. We had obtained a saddle horse apiece and a packhorse from the ranger station near Superior, Montana, and made about twelve miles up the creek and camped about dark at an old placer mining cabin on Trout Creek.

By the time we were unpacked it was dark, and I made a palouser from a tin can and a candle, and we started to look for water. Jim was carrying the water bucket ahead of me, and the path crossed an old mining flume with a plank laid across it. Just at the middle the plank broke, and Jim was precipitated to the bottom of the flume, four or five feet. He fell heavily and struck his shoulder on a stake or other projection. When I got him back to camp and the light of the fire and removed his shirt, it was obvious that he had dislocated his shoulder joint. I had some recollection that such a dislocation could be pulled back in place, and took off my boot and tried pulling with my foot in his armpit. Jim was a heavily muscled man, and after torturing him a while with my unskilled efforts I gave it up. He was in great pain, but I did my best to make him comfortable with a good bough bed beside the fire.

I did not want to leave him alone during the cold of the night, but at gray of dawn I saddled Roy Phillip's tough, hard-gaited bay horse and started down the trail at his best speed. I think I never rode a rough trail as fast as that, and by the time I got to Superior the bay was a lather of foam from head to tail. I got hold of a doctor, called Roy Phillips at the ranger station, and four of us started back up the trail, but it was nearly noon when we got to the camp. Jim was still on the bed suffering much pain, but too tough and proud to complain about it. The doctor laid him on a table in the old cabin, chloroformed him, and pulled the shoulder back in place and strapped it up. When Jim came out of the anesthetic the doctor poured a stiff shot of whiskey into him, and Jim got to his feet and led us all down the trail twelve miles to Superior without stopping. He not only had the dislocated shoulder, but the nerve at the point of his elbow had been smashed, and he must have suffered exquisite pain, but he was and still is as tough as they make them.

When the United States entered the First World War in 1917, naturally most of us foresters of military age expected to get into it. We felt, and quite rightly, that our experience as woodsmen and mountain men, and our practice in handling and organizing large bodies of men on forest fires should make us good soldiers. But the powers that be had other ideas. Our chief, Henry S. Graves, very promptly sent out directions that we should sit tight. It was hard for a young man to take, but he was probably right in his belief that a limited number of foresters could do more for the war by the exercise of their technical ability than as fighting men. Wood in many forms and in sufficient quantity is one of the essentials of modern war, and the Forest Service could do much to help on the wood problem.[11]

There were three principal lines in which the Forest Service could be useful: First to maintain the protection of the national forests, particularly against the danger of incendiary fires, and to make the national forest timber available for use in the war. Somebody had to stay home to handle this job. Then there was the big field of wood technology. The Forest Service, with its forest products laboratory at Madison, Wisconsin, knew more about wood than any other agency, and almost inevitably it was called on to advise the army and navy on a great many technical questions on the uses and availability of wood for various military purposes—such things as design and fabrication of laminated wooden airplane propellers, plywood airplane fuselages, walnut for gunstocks, oak for army wagons, quick kiln-drying of wood for all the many purposes for which vast supplies were needed immediately, and the training of army and navy inspectors in acquiring wood products.[12] All these and many similar activities immediately engaged the wood technologists of the Forest Service, and the organization had to be expanded many times.

The third big activity was help and advice to the army in forming the 10th Regiment of Forest Engineers to log and saw timber in France for the invading American army.[13] This forestry regiment was largely a Forest Service baby. It was officered in large part by Forest Service men or men selected by the Forest Service through its intimate contact with the lumber industry.

My first war activity as a forest supervisor was to guard the critical bridges on the two transcontinental railroads traversing my forest. There was much talk about probable German sabotage, and the possible blowing up of the high bridges, which might tie up an important railroad for weeks. The Forest Service being already on the ground could get action much quicker than the army, so at the request of the army I immediately put out three or four three-man bridge guards, armed with rifles, at some of the high trestles on the Northern Pacific and Milwaukee Railroads. It seemed a little bit like playing soldier, but the army considered it of

FIG. 17. Elers Koch as forest supervisor, circa 1912.

enough importance so that in a few weeks our Forest Service guards were replaced by soldiers for the duration of the war.

It was hard for me to settle down to timber sales and fire fighting and the routine of forest administration through the summer of 1917. I felt like a slacker for not being in the war, but had to obey orders from the chief. Finally in the late fall of that year I got my chance. Mr. Graves wired me that he was recommending me to the army for a commission as major in the 10th Regiment, and I was instructed to proceed to Fort Yellowstone at Mammoth Springs in Yellowstone Park for physical examination. Geographically it may have been the nearest army post, but it was the devil of a place to get to in the winter when the park was closed to travel.

I took the N. P. to Livingstone, and a branch line to Gardiner, which is about ten miles from the post. There were no regular stages running at this season, but I caught a ride in an army truck. Arriving at Mammoth Springs late in the evening, I found that there were no hotels or other accommodations open, but my G. I. truck driver kindly directed me to a sergeant's house where he thought I might be put up. The sergeant proved amenable, and incidentally I saved his house from burning up that night. The sergeant and his wife went off to a post dance, leaving me alone in the house. Shortly after I went to bed I smelled smoke, and got up to investigate. The sergeant's wife in her hurry to get a dress pressed for the dance had gone off leaving an electric iron on the ironing board with the current on, and it had nearly burned through the board when I discovered it.

In the morning I proceeded to the military headquarters. Nobody seemed to take much interest in my quest, and I had considerable difficulty locating the post surgeon. I began to think this was a pretty poor reception for an incipient major, but I finally got hold of the doctor, who took me into a cold, unheated room where I stripped for examination, shivering, and covered with goose pimples from the cold. The doctor gave me a routine examination and after I had resumed my clothes announced that I had failed to pass the physical examination. He said I had a bad lung and never could stand the hardships of war. I had never heard of such a thing, and offered to walk down any officer at the post if they would take me on, but my protests were of no avail. There never was anything wrong with my lungs. I have since had several examinations by civilian doctors and they found no such indication. I have always thought my rejection was because I am quite round shouldered, and the doctor thought I would not look well in a uniform, and let me down easy by an alleged lung infection. At any rate that ended my hope for a military career.

The next spring I got orders to go in to Washington for a detail in the Forest Service on war activities. I was made a sort of general assistant to Earl Clapp, who had charge of all the Forest Service research work on wood products in cooperation with the army.[14] I did a little of everything: personnel, appointments, finance, and general errand-boy work in following up leads of possibilities for the Forest Service to be of use in the war. I often had errands in the old State War and Navy building, and followed its corridors endlessly looking for the right man to contact. I never did succeed in getting out the same door whereby I entered, nor did I ever know what street I would emerge on till I got my bearings outside. I hope I was of some use to Clapp, who was extremely busy and much overworked, but by fall I had all of Washington I cared for. I wanted in the worst way to get home to Montana and my family, and the Armistice had not been signed two days when I was on the train headed west.

Now I was not sorry to try a new job, and in 1919 I was transferred to the regional office as fire chief. I spent two hard years on that job, and in 1921 became assistant regional forester in charge of the Division of Timber Management.[15]

I stayed in that job till my retirement in the spring of 1944.

CHAPTER 4

Forest Fires

The year of a forester in the western districts is divided into two parts—the forest fire season, and the rest of the year. In a bad fire season—from the first of July until the September rains—one lives, breathes, and thinks nothing but fire, and a good part of the balance of the year is spent in making plans and preparations for the next fire season.

I have often wondered how it is possible there is any timber left in the western mountains when one thinks of the thousands of years since the last glacial epoch, when lightning and Indian-set fires ran unchecked, with no protective organization. In the fairly wet years the loss is small; the big acreage burned comes intermittently in real drought years. In my time as a forester in this region I have lived through at least nine years which could be classed as really bad forest fire years: 1910, 1914, 1917, 1919, 1925, 1926, 1929, 1931, and 1934.

It is well known that drought years come in cycles, and without much doubt my contemporaries and I lived through a fire period which may not occur again in equal intensity for a hundred years. It started off with a bang in the historic year of 1910, when fire swept the Northwest from end to end, culminating in the terrific blowup of August 21, when in this region, eighty-five lives were lost besides the destruction of several towns, mines, ranches, and livestock, and millions of acres of forest land were left a blackened waste. It was a complete defeat for the newly organized Forest Service forces, but the story has been told so many times in magazine articles and books that it will not be repeated here.[1]

Not only was there the immediate loss, but it is a well-known fact that fire breeds fire, and for many years the 1910 burns, with their inflammable dead material, were a constant threat to the rest of the forest. It is only of late years that, with the snags mostly down, and a new growth of trees springing up on many of the burns, that the 1910 burns are becoming a protectable area. Much of the area was burned a second time in the succeeding series of bad fire years, and it is on these doubly burned areas that most of the tree planting in Montana and Idaho has been done, and with very satisfying results. As forest supervisor I naturally had my share of fire fighting, and I usually tried to get out on all the larger fires, and as many of the small ones as possible. As regional fire chief in 1919 and 1920 I went from one bad fire situation to another all over western Montana and northern Idaho, particularly in 1919, which was almost as bad a fire year as 1910. Later, as chief of the Division of Timber Management, fire was not my main job, but as every man in the service has to contribute his share during a bad season, and as I had acquired some reputation as a fire fighter, I frequently found myself in charge of operations on some of the worst fires.

Fire fighting is perhaps the nearest thing there is to war, and not without its danger, and always requires extreme physical exertion, long hours, lack of sleep, and constant nervous tension. Moving in on a fire which has gone beyond control with a crew of men, when one looks up toward the destination and sees an enormous threatening thunderhead crowding up into the sky, indicating a wild crown fire, it is understandable that one sometimes has a feeling of butterflies in his stomach. In a way it is like troops moving in to the front line and listening to the artillery and shell bursts ahead.

FIG. 18. Down timber in a heavy stand of western white pine following the 1910 wildfire on the Little North Fork of the St. Joe River, St. Joe National Forest. R. H. McKay photo, U.S. Forest Service.

If I have had any success in controlling big fires, it is because I have never believed in generalship from the rear, but always tried to be in the most critical spots at the most critical times. With a fire camp of, say one hundred men, it is breakfast before daylight, and mighty cold it is too, then moving the crews out on the fire line at the first gray of dawn, perhaps to relieve a small night crew. I usually went out with the fire crews, saw them properly placed to extend the fire lines, gave my instructions to the foremen, and then proceeded to scout ahead to see what the fire was doing and plan the operation. Scouting a fire is hard and often dangerous work involving much walking and climbing through the toughest kind of topography, brush thickets, and down timber. I used to figure on wearing out completely one set of boot soles and hobnails in a season. Sometimes one could get inside the burned area for easier going, jumping from blackened log to log, and avoiding still-hot ashes and coals, and with the ever-present danger of some burning snag crashing on one's head. When scouting outside the burned area there is always danger of getting caught in the sudden uprush of a crown fire, and many a breathless climb have I had escaping such a thrust.

In the afternoon I usually tried to get back on the fire lines where I figured the main battle would occur, holding the lines already constructed during the heat and wind of the afternoon. Falling snags are the greatest danger in working along the fire line. On fires in which I have taken part, at least six or eight men have been killed by burning snags crashing down on them, and it is not a pretty sight to see a man with his head smashed and the brains spilling out. It is extremely demoralizing to a crew, and after such an accident one always expects a big walkout of men the next morning.

I recall one particularly fierce battle in the Hemlock Creek fire on the Clearwater Forest. The fire, which was largely in dead timber, had blown up almost immediately after the lightning strike. Trail crews and other available men were moved in from all directions. I happened to be on an inspection trip in the forest, and seeing the burst of smoke from thirty miles away, I knew it was a bad situation and headed for the fire as fast as my horse could take me. I went in with a fire camp under

Ranger Jim Diehl on the lower point of the fire, and camp was set in a cedar flat about half a mile below the fire edge.[2] Since the wind was carrying the blaze down the creek, we undertook first to cut it off on the lower side. The first day a line was partially completed around the lower edge of the fire, but unfortunately it was necessary to locate the line on a steep slope with the fire breaking down from above, which is always a hard line to hold.

The following afternoon we had one of the hardest battles I have ever encountered on a fire. The dead timber stand was heavy, with giant white pines 150 feet high, and much half-rotten hemlock and white fir to throw sparks. In midafternoon the humidity dropped and the wind blew, and the fire really raged. Our puny fifteen-foot-wide line below it seemed a very slim defense. We stopped constructing any new line, and all hands were concentrated at the danger points to hold what we had. Dry logs on the fire side of the line were blazing wildly, and every man with a shovel was throwing dirt desperately to try to damp down the fierceness of the blaze. Burning snags were falling constantly, and the position was one of the greatest danger. Of course I couldn't work the crew in such a spot without staying close with them, but my heart was in my mouth every time I heard a snag crack. One tremendous dead white pine, four feet through and perhaps 160 or 170 feet tall, was all ablaze, and everyone was watching it. It started to topple. "Look out! Here it comes!" and the crew scattered both ways along the fire line. Down it came with a thunderous crash that shook the earth, and slid down the mountainside, top first, in a cloud of dust and smoke, across our fire line, and stopped a hundred feet below. Of course it carried fire of all sorts with it. I got the scared crew together, and working desperately with saws and mattocks, we looped a line down around it. Scarcely had we completed this line when another snag came plunging across the line a hundred yards away. Again I rallied the worn-out crew, and again we looped a line around the break. But it was no use. A third and a fourth snag came down. The line was clearly untenable. Fires were burning wildly on both sides, and it was apparent that there was a general blowup. The foremen and I got the crew together, checked to see that we had the last man, and retreated down the mountain toward camp.

The fire was raging so violently, and moving so fast down the creek, that Jim Diehl and I agreed we could not hold the camp. It was then about seven o'clock in the evening. We had a crew of about one hundred men, and for safety sent them a couple of miles down the creek with their bedrolls, under a foreman, to await developments. Diehl and I decided to bury the camp. We had ten or twelve men and put them to work digging trenches. Into these we piled grub, dishes, tools, canvas flies, and all the other camp paraphernalia, but before we shoveled the dirt back in, Jim said, "Let's make one more try to save the camp." A gasoline-powered pump and two or three hundred feet of hose had just been brought in that evening, and Jim got that to working. The fire was all around us, lighting up the darkness, and every little while one of us would say, "We better get down the trail while we can," but the other would be so busy throwing water he would say, "Let's wait just a little more." Finally the cool of night worked in our favor, and we had the camp pretty safe. The next morning we got a couple of mule strings in and moved the camp down the creek. We had to start all over again, but we were glad we had not shoveled dirt on top of all that camp outfit.

Gasoline pumps and hose are pretty handy in certain spots. At one time it was thought that they would revolutionize fire fighting, but I have found them useful mainly in holding an occasional hot spot or saving a camp. I remember one occasion with amusement. It was on the big Slate Creek fire on the St. Joe. I had one big camp on one side of the fire, and had been there a full week, gradually shoving the fire back. It was late September and the nights were cold. That was before we had the new kapok sleeping bags, and two single government blankets make a pretty slim bed. One night the fire broke over one of the lines and backed down on the camp so that it was nearly encircled in a steadily advancing blaze. We had a pump in camp, and I heard Jack Root, the district ranger, get up and route out a dozen men. Soon I heard the steady hum of the pump and the hiss of water. I thought, "Well, Jack is doing everything that needs to be done," and settled back in the blankets. The circle of fire warmed the whole camp, and I had the only four or five hours of good warm sleep that I had put in on that job.

Everyone who has fought big fires for thirty years has inevitably had a number of what seemed like narrow escapes from death. Working up close to a hot fire, one faces danger from falling snags or being caught in a sudden rush of the fire. Scouting around a fire, usually alone, involves a continual risk of being cut off in a bad place.

As I look back on my experience, it seems to me that the tightest spot I was ever in developed on the Slate Creek fire in 1934 on the St. Joe Forest. The fire had been going several days when I arrived at Avery. I obtained a saddle horse and rode up the trail to the lookout on Flash Peak. A CCC crew was camped here in charge of one of the camp superintendents. I can't recall his name. I sent my horse back to Avery with a CCC boy and went down to look over the situation.

I found the fire line that had just been completed by this camp and another camp in Slate Creek down a draw to the main Slate Creek, about two miles. The line was in contact with the fire near the summit of the mountain, but gradually diverged from the fire edge and paralleled the draw down to the main creek, about one-third of the way up on the south slope. The fire had checked, for the most part at the bottom of the draw, but it was all set for another run, and it was immediately evident to me that this line could not be held if the fire were permitted to burn up to it with an uphill drag.

It was the middle of the afternoon when I went down the line with the superintendent. I was afraid to start backfiring that afternoon, but told him to start near the top of the mountain as early as possible next morning, and backfire down the line as fast as he could, expecting to carry the backfire as fast as possible all the way down to Slate Creek. I went on down the line and spent the night at the Slate Creek camp.

Next morning I started out with Harry Gisborne.[3] Just before I left Slate Creek, Gisborne took the relative humidity with a sling psychrometer. He gave me a reading, which showed fairly high humidity, and I drew what turned out to be a wrong conclusion that we could expect a fairly favorable day so far as burning conditions went.

Frank Bishop had charge of the crew from the Slate Creek camp, and together with him and his crew we climbed up the fire line till we met the superintendent near the top of the mountain. It was now the middle of the morning, and I was dismayed to find that he had not even started backfiring as I had ordered. I had figured that the backfire would be halfway down by that time. I am afraid I lost my temper and berated him rather severely. It was now pretty late to start backfiring, but I knew the line could not possibly be held any other way and started his crew to work at once, setting a good deal of the fire myself.

After a couple of hours, when the fires were going good, I started down the line to see what was happening below. Bishop, having heard my "cussing out" of the superintendent, had apparently made up his mind he was going to do his share, and had started enthusiastically backfiring the lower part of the line. I had not counted on that, as I wanted to work the backfire down from above, so we would always have a getaway route. It was a dry south slope, densely covered with brush and interspersed with down logs and snags. The backfire was burning pretty hard, and the main fire at the bottom of the draw was beginning to stir. It didn't look too good to me, and as I went down the line observing it I discovered that the backfire below me had jumped the line and was making a run for the ridge top. Half of Bishop's crew had withdrawn below the break and about forty men remained with me in charge of Ranger Stan Larson. I figured we had better be looking for a getaway, and we started back up the fire line. To my dismay the fire had also jumped the line above us and was raging toward the mountaintop in heavy dead timber. The superintendent had withdrawn his crew over the mountain.

So here we were on a section of perhaps a quarter of a mile of unburned fire line with the fire across, both above and below us. We moved down toward the lower end, and I found a small ridge where the backfire had run out perhaps two hundred feet below the fire line. We moved out on to that, but the ground was still hot and smoking and our island of safety seemed mighty small and precarious. I could see that the whole gulch was going out in a few minutes in a big burst of fire, and our chances of surviving such a general conflagration seemed small. Things looked pretty bleak, and I figured next day Bishop would be sifting forty heaps of ashes for our buttons. The men were uneasy but quiet. I got Larson aside for a consultation. In the dense smoke we had no way of telling how wide the belt of fire was below us. It might be a hundred yards, or it could be half a mile. Larson said he didn't think we could stick it out where we were and thought we might make a run down the line through the fire, which was advancing up both sides of the fire line toward us.

It seemed like a counsel of desperation, but it was better to try something. So I said I would take the lead if he would come behind the crew. The fire was blazing hot in the brush and logs on both sides of the fire line, so I put my arm over my face as a shield and dashed into it, the men close behind me. The heat and smoke were terrific, but there was no turning back, and a three-hundred-yard run brought me out to where I could see clear sky through the smoke. I was never so glad to see anything in my life. If it had been much farther we couldn't have made it.

We all got through safely and found Bishop and his men waiting below, wondering what had become of us. My eyes were so smoked up I could hardly see, and as the whole gulch was going out with a roar, there was nothing we could do till it checked on the ridge top and we could get near the fire. So I pulled the whole crew down to Slate Creek and spent the whole day putting wet cloths on my burning eyes. The next morning, as I expected, the fire checked on the ridge, and a day's work by both crews pretty well sewed it up. I have had a mighty high regard for Stan Larson ever since, and figure his judgment saved the lives of forty men.

Of all the many causes of forest fires, lightning in this region is the most serious. This is because lightning fires so often occur in inaccessible and remote spots where it takes time to get men on them. Man-caused fires are at least apt to be accessible by road or trail. Constant educational effort has somewhat reduced the number of man-caused fires, but it is incredible how much carelessness still exists which results in fires from smokers, campfires, or ill-advised land-clearing operations. But of all the man-caused fires the ones that are most infuriating to the forester are the incendiary fires—ones that are deliberately set. That class of fires has greatly diminished in number in recent years, but in the early days of the Forest Service they were quite common, sometimes to create employment at fire fighting, or often from general cussedness.

I remember particularly the worst epidemic of incendiary fires we ever had, which occurred in the Kootenai Forest in northwestern Montana. In what was known as the Pinkham Ridge country there was a settlement of West Virginia mountaineers. They were the same type as the well-known Southern mountaineer families, and had imported most of their prejudices and customs with them. Most of them had only a small clearing of agricultural land, inadequate to support a family, and made a living as they did in the South by cutting railroad ties and moonshining. They were a reserved and isolated race, and resented any outside interference.

We had for some years had occasional trouble with them and strongly suspected them of setting fires deliberately. In 1919, a bad fire year, we had a regular epidemic of incendiary fires in the Pinkham Ridge country. As fast as the Forest Service could put out one fire, new fires would spring up, till they had the rangers and smoke chasers run ragged. I never could see any logical reason for it, but it looked as though the young men of that community were playing a game with the Forest Service, largely for devilment. The supervisor was more or less at his wit's end, and a couple of us from the regional office went up to confer with him. As we met at Eureka we could look up and see the long profile of Pinkham Ridge. Strung along the top of the ridge about a quarter of a mile apart, six or eight smoke columns were spiraling up. It was obvious that someone had ridden along the ridge and freshly set a series of fires. The supervisor, Art Baum, was thoroughly discouraged.

"What can we do?" he said. "They can set fires faster than we can put them out. I think we had better pull out and let the Pinkham Ridge country burn. Maybe the Pinkham Ridgers will find they have too much fire."

After discussing the matter for a while, I made a proposal. "Those Pinkham Ridge people," I said, "don't understand anything except force. If we put on a show of superior force, maybe they will back down." So I proposed that we gather up half a dozen of our best and toughest old forest rangers and put them in to patrol that country, armed to the teeth, and make a considerable show of it. We got together six rangers, men like Frank Hahn and Fred Ainger, who had been in the mountains most of their lives. Each man had a Winchester on his saddle and a six-shooter on his hip. They moved into camp in the heart of the Pinkham Ridge country and proceeded to patrol the trails in pairs. Of course the mountaineers could easily have evaded them and set fires just the same, but they were getting too much publicity and outside notice; it interfered with the moonshining business for one thing. And so the old patriarch of the colony called off the young fellows from their deviltry. The first night one of them sent a bullet through the rangers' tent, but after that they settled down, and we never had any more trouble from that community.

The modern Forest Service has things pretty well organized and cooperative action worked out so that it is usually possible to get organized competent fire crews from logging camps, mines, and the like, but in the earlier days of the Service we had to gather together such men as we could get from the streets, the saloons, and off the freight train. As a result there was almost as much misery from handling the men as with fighting the forest fire. Such transients were almost like children—unreasonable, irresponsible, and acting purely on impulse. They had absolutely no feeling of obligation or responsibility to their employers, which was perhaps natural, since few employers of that time felt any responsibility toward them. Time and again a whole crew would walk out at a critical time for some trivial reason. If we were lucky there would be enough good lumberjacks in a crew to fill the axe and saw gangs, and the punks and stew bums would be given a shovel or mattock to get the best they could out of it. I remember an old ranger calling me on the phone saying a fire had broken over badly and he needed some men right away. "How many do you need," I asked. "Send me ten men if they wear hats; if they wear caps I'll need thirty." The distinction was that the respectable lumberjack never wears a cap in summer, always a felt hat, usually a black one, whereas the pool-hall boys and general stew bums, in those days, usually wore caps and shoved their hands deep in their pockets.

In the early days before the Forest Service had developed as good fiscal facilities as they have now, the paying off of fire crews was always a problem. Few of the men had a cent in their pockets when they came on a fire, nor did most of them have any permanent address to which a check could be sent. They wanted their money right away, and we had to give them at least part of their pay before we could release them. In 1910 I happened to have three or four hundred dollars in the bank, and Frank Hahn, one of my rangers, had about the same. I borrowed $500 from F. A. Silcox, the assistant district forester, and we must have turned that $1,000 over a dozen times during the fire season.[4] I would pay the men in cash or by personal check, get a receipt, and turn in an expense account, which was put through as quickly as possible so I could turn the money over again. I was finally made a temporary disbursing agent, so I could draw government funds in advance to pay off a crew. I remember one time I went over to Wallace to help pay off a fire crew. The bank was closed when I got there, but we got hold of the president, and he cashed a government check for me after hours. I had over $1,000 in silver, currency, and gold—largely gold—stacked up on a table upstairs in the supervisor's office. The men had been waiting for hours for their pay and were pretty restless and impatient. We let them up the stairs one or two at a time, and I started to pay off the time slips. I wasn't much used to handling cash in quantity, especially gold, and was a bit nervous about it. The first two men each had twelve or thirteen dollars coming, and I gave them a gold piece and the rest in silver. Then I realized to my dismay that I had got mixed up in my gold pieces and had given each of them a twenty-dollar gold piece instead of a ten, but it was too late; they were off down the stairs and into the street. I had to stand the $20 loss myself, which was quite something for a man getting $2,000 a year.

In the early nineteen hundreds working men in this region usually carried their own bedrolls, which resulted in most logging and construction bunkhouses being infected with both lice and bedbugs. I remember once in 1910 I hired a crew from the Missoula streets to go on a fire near Frenchtown. I asked each man as I signed him on if he had a bed, and all said they had. So I arranged for a wagon to meet the train at Frenchtown to carry the bedrolls. But when we disembarked from the train there were only two bedrolls to go in the wagon—my own and the cook's. We fought fire all day, and at night I had the men build up a good big campfire of logs. Of course they did not get much sleep, and most of them sat up all night by the fire, talking mostly about the relative merits of the different jails they had been in. After that we bought up all the cheap sougans and shoddy blankets we could find in the local stores, and gave each man one. The fire bed was shortly after standardized as two army blankets and a canvas tarp for each man, but it was not until we got modern kapok sleeping bags that a man could get a decent night's sleep on a fire job.

It seems to me that there is far less drunkenness among casual working men nowadays than there was thirty or more years ago. When we loaded a crew of fire fighters on the train we always expected most of them to be drunk, and consequently hard to handle. One night in 1910 we were shipping out all the men we could scrape up from Missoula for fires to the west. I had fifty to get off at Frenchtown, and Walt Derrick was taking another fifty through to Avery. We had not yet worked out the system of hat checks we used later, but assembled the men and counted them as well as we could at the railroad station, and both Walt and I bought tickets for the number of men we thought we had. The men piled on the train, and being mostly drunk, promptly went to sleep. Along came the conductor and we showed him the tickets. He said, "Now come along and show me which are your men." "Hell," I said, "We can't tell which are our men; some of them are and some of them are other working men." The conductor raged up and down the aisle for a while, but most of the men were asleep, and did not know where they were going anyhow. So he gave up in disgust and growled, "Give me your tickets and they can all ride." When we got to Frenchtown, I could not tell which were my men and which Walt's, so I shoved off about fifty of the men who were awake, and so got the best of Walt, for he got the worst drunks.

The IWW (Industrial Workers of the World) movement among Northwest lumberjacks reached its height between 1917 and 1919. These were both exceptionally bad fire years, but men were unusually available for fire fighting since most of the lumber camps were shut down by the intermittent strikes. The men would work for the government, but not for the lumber companies. Our district forester at that time, F. A. Silcox, who afterwards became chief forester, was accused of being a Wobbly himself. Certainly he had a great deal of sympathy for the movement. This feeling was shared by many Forest Service men, in spite of the unreasonableness of men in the movement and the difficulty of handling such men. They had many just complaints against the lumber companies. Living conditions in many of the logging camps were very bad, and the demands of the men for clean camps and clean beds were well justified. In a report describing conditions in one camp, my old check scaler, Skip Knouf, made the statement that the only time it was safe to go to the latrine was at mealtime, when all the flies were in the cookhouse.[5]

Labor conditions were particularly difficult in 1919. The Wobblies, including many of the foremen, practically took control of fire camps. Along the fire lines the fresh-cut log ends were decorated with a big IWW or a crude picture of a black cat sitting on an axe handle. Men were forced to take out a red card or get out of camp. One time I pulled in to a large fire camp of about 150 men near Lolo Springs. Owing to shortage of forest officers I had put in charge a foreman well recommended to me, but a known Wobbly. I found the work was going badly and the foreman incompetent, and promptly fired him. He retired to the camp and in half an hour came back and said, "If I go out, all the men are going out with me." The fire situation was critical, and the loss of the whole crew would be disastrous, but I stood my ground and told him, "All right, we will have their time made out in the morning, but according to the contract the men, and that includes yourself, get no time or expenses to and from the fire."

The men were in an ugly humor, and I expected trouble, as we were forty miles from town. I called up my office and asked that they send out what cars they could hire to take the men to town in the morning, and also suggested they send a deputy sheriff along. I worked half the night with the timekeepers making out the time slips, and on each one we deducted the cost of the ride to town, besides half a day's travel time each way. Rather to my surprise the men got off in the morning without too much trouble, and the gods were with us, for that day it settled down to rain so hard that we did not have to replace the crew.

Occasionally we had to use violent methods. One time I had a fire camp on Snow Creek in Idaho. We had been there for a long tedious fight of ten days, gradually crowding a stubborn fire out of Snow Creek. Every morning, as usual, there were from three to half a dozen men demanding their time. One morning about twenty of them decided to go down the road. I got the fire crews out under two foremen, and stayed in camp myself till the men could be started down the trail. They kept crowding around the timekeeper, who was working as fast as he could to make out the time. I walked up to the group and said, "Get back, men; you are just interfering with the work." They paid not the slightest attention to me and continued arguing with the timekeeper. I was really mad and walked over to a pile of mattocks and slipped the handle from one. I shoved back into the group and repeated, "Now get back. I told you the timekeeper can't work with you crowding around." Most of them fell back grumbling, but one bristly faced Irishman thrust his face into mine and growled, "Aw to hell with you." I hit him as hard as I could across the upper arm. I thought I had broken his arm but I didn't care. He retreated cursing and howling, holding his damaged arm, while I stalked over to my bedroll and sat down glumly, still holding my weapon. When the timekeeper finished the time slips, I ok'd them, taking my time about it, and the men went down the trail with no further trouble. A pick handle makes a pretty good persuader, even for a small man. I am somewhat ashamed of losing my temper, and never did tell the story to anyone.

Fire control methods have greatly improved since the early days. Not only are fire crews better organized and equipped, but the whole process of detecting small fires and getting to them quickly has been greatly stepped up. When we started fire fighting on a big scale in 1910 we had little equipment available, and we bought axes, shovels, saws, mattocks, dishes, and a sougan apiece for the men until we exhausted the supply in

FIG. 19. (*above*) Manned lookout towers were critical to fire control efforts in the 1920s and 1930s. (*opposite*) Each tower was equipped with a "seen-area" map board and a Koch alidade to ascertain compass bearing and distance to lightning strikes, smokes, and fires. K. D. Swan photos, U.S. Forest Service.

the region. Naturally it was a job packing such a miscellaneous outfit on pack animals, and we gradually evolved more standardized outfits, mostly in twenty-five-man units. Instead of a miscellaneous mess of dishes and boilers the whole mess outfit was neatly packed in two boilers, each of which made a side pack for a mule. Axes, mattocks, and shovels and all other equipment were crated ready for packing. Two big district ware-houses were established, one in Spokane and one in Missoula. Nowadays if a supervisor needs equipment for a hundred-man fire, he calls up one of the warehouses, and by express or truck, out come four fine twenty-five-man outfits, all ready to load on a pack string, and complete to the last detail, besides special emergency rations for the first three days. If he needs more pack stock than he has available, he calls the remount depot near Missoula, and in fifteen minutes a complete string of nine mules and a saddle horse, with all equipment and a packer, are roaring off at fifty miles an hour in specially built trucks.

Since I retired four years ago, even more new developments have occurred through the use of airplanes, and on an inaccessible small fire two or four, or even twenty-five or thirty smoke jumpers are parachuting from the skies, followed by tools and grub. What a difference from the old days!

CHAPTER 5

The Lochsa River Fire

A forester in the Northwest dates the events of his life by fire years. The 1910, 1917, 1919, 1926, 1929, and 1931 fire seasons each have a character of their own, and in each year there are individual fire campaigns which the forester remembers as the soldier recalls the separate engagements of a war.

The Lochsa River fire in 1929 is one that I recall most vividly. It stands out as one of the longest, hardest-fought campaigns in my personal experience, and its location in one of the most inaccessible and primitive regions of the United States added to the usual vicissitudes of fire fighting.

On the night of August 1, a sudden mountain thunderstorm reverberated through the Lochsa River Canyon.[1] Chenowith and Larson, the smoke chaser and lookout at Castle Butte, sat in the glass-walled lookout house and took the bearing of each lightning stroke that seemed to reach the ground.[2] By daylight they had spotted three smokes, and at 4:10 Chenowith set out with his backpack of forty-one pounds of grub and tools for the nearest smoke down Bald Mountain Creek. When he reached the fire at 6:30 it had already covered three-quarters of an acre. A big dead cedar had been struck by the lightning bolt and scattered

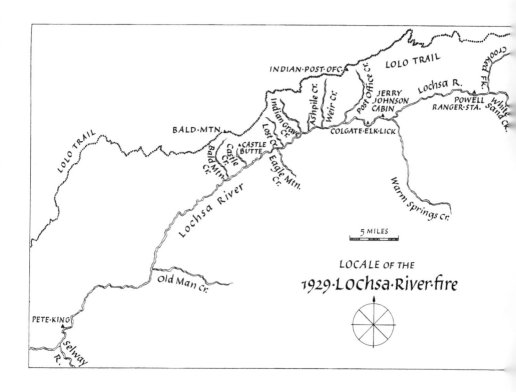

FIG. 20. Locale of the 1929 Lochsa River fire, which had its origins in the Bald Mountain Creek on the north side of the Lochsa River and near Old Man Creek south of the river. The fire moved northeast up the river and was finally checked near Post Office Creek and Colgate Springs on the north side of the river and near Warm Springs Creek on the south side.

burning fragments in all directions. Chenowith laid down his pack and set to work with axe and mattock to cut and trench a line around the fire, which was burning in heavy down logs. About the middle of the afternoon a high wind came up and in spite of his best efforts the fire blew across his line and made a run up the hill. The lookout was watching, and when the smoke commenced to roll up, he called for reinforcements. Men came from all directions, from the district trail camp and lookout. Case, the assistant ranger, and two men came up from the Lochsa Station. Three trail men came in from the Eagle Mountain Trail, and three from Fish Creek. By seven the next morning there were nine men on the fire. The pack string from the Lochsa Station brought in supplies and placed the fire camp at a spring on the hillside half a mile above the fire. Again in the afternoon the dry southwest wind blew a gale. The fire scattered from rotten snags and swept up the slope gathering intensity and velocity. The camp was burned, the cook barely getting out with his life. The men fell back to the river, a new camp and more men were brought in, and a fresh attack made.

On the 7th, I was just completing an inspection trip on the Clearwater Forest when instructions came from the Missoula office for me to check on fire conditions on the Selway. The Bald Mountain fire was reported out of control, and a serious situation was developing in Old Man Creek.

I left my car at Pete King, the main supply depot at the junction of the Lochsa and Selway Rivers. Here the assembling forces were gathering pack strings, and truckload after truckload of food supply and tools were coming in from Spokane. I rode thirty miles on horseback to the fire camp at the mouth of Bald Mountain Creek. Forest Supervisor Wolff was in charge in person, with a crew of about fifty men. That afternoon I scouted the fire sufficiently to obtain a general idea of the situation. The fire had burned down the creek nearly to the river and had covered about three-quarters of the Bald Mountain Creek drainage. Fire lines had been extended some distance up the ridges on either side of the creek and were holding successfully. About two miles back from the river, the fire in its terrific rush to the ridge top had spattered spots of fire well down into Castle Creek, the next drainage to the east. Wolff and I both agreed that this was the critical point. If it could be controlled it was probable that the fire could be held to the Bald Mountain Creek drainage.

The crew was out before daylight the next morning. The plan was for Ranger Hand with twenty men to continue the fire line up the west ridge. Townsend, with a pump crew, was to attack a heavy fire in the creek bottom, which threatened to back down the creek to the river, and Bill McRoberts, a trail crew foreman, was to take twenty men up the east ridge and drop down to the fire on Castle Creek. A new camp was to be established at the Castle Butte lookout, and Bill's men were to be brought up there for the night. I decided to scout the fire in the upper part of Bald Mountain Creek. I started up the east ridge and then cut through on a contour across the freshly burned area into Bald Mountain Creek. The slope showed evidence of a terrific blast of fire. Every tree was charred black, and the fire had swept the ground like a blowtorch, utterly consuming every particle of vegetable matter so that the soil on the steep slopes was a shifting black desert of granite sand and ashes which slid and trickled under my feet. The ground was still hot, with many logs burning and snags crashing down at intervals. I pushed my way across the burn as rapidly as possible, and with my eyes cocked for dangerous snags, slipping and sliding on the steep ground. It was a blistering hot day, and it made a long hard half-day's trip before I reached the upper edge of the fire. It was moving steadily in dead timber up the creek, blazing high in places where the fuel was heavy. I picked a quiet sector and managed to get across the live fire edge to the unburned ground.

It was a long pull from here up to the Lolo Trail at the summit, and I was more than glad when I hit the trail to intercept two pack strings headed for Castle Butte. Fortunately, one string had a spare bell mare without a pack, and I gratefully climbed aboard bareback for the five miles of steep trail to the lookout. A fire camp was established at the lookout, and Bill's men pulled in late, pretty well done up from the long climb.

The next morning I went down with the crew to the critical point on Castle Creek. The fire had spotted over the ridge in a long tongue, extending almost down to the creek between two lateral branches. It was burning fiercely at the lower end in heavy dead timber, but I hoped that if we cut it off at the bottom, the branch creeks would temporarily hold the fire from spreading laterally along the slope until we could extend fire lines from the bottom up to the ridge along the flanks of the fire. If I had had fifty men instead of twenty I believe we could have made it. Burning conditions could not have been worse, with heavy dead timber killed in the 1910 fires, and grown up to dense brush. The timber was mostly white fir and cedar. Rotten white fir snags would catch fire in the tops and throw showers of sparks which again and again blew across our fire line and started fires in rotten wood back of the line. Big hollow dead cedars came crashing down across the line, shattered into kindling wood, and burst into flames. The falling snags were a constant hazard to the men. A 150-foot dead tree comes down with a slam that shakes the ground like the burst of a high-explosive shell, and is calculated to put fear into the hearts of the bravest crew of men.

From the feel of the air I knew it was going to be an exceptionally bad fire day. About two o'clock I climbed up on a rocky point on the far side of the creek where I could overlook the fire. The flames were everywhere picking up in volume and intensity. Even as I watched, the fire crossed the small creek just above our fire line and swept up the slope, great masses of flaming gas rolling out of the black smoke and whole areas bursting into flame spontaneously. Next I saw it cross the other fork and cut off our way back to camp. I still sat for five minutes looking down at the crew working on the fire line, thinking what a pitiful effort man can exert when the great forces of nature are really aroused. Two men were working below me with canvas water buckets. A tall white fir crashed down immediately over them. The two men dived under a protecting creek bank and came up out of a cloud of dust and smoke, looking scared and foolish. A group of men were watching a big hollow cedar close to the fire line that was burning like a chimney. Down it came across the creek, scattering flaming kindling in all directions.

I saw that the jig was up and the best we could do was get out without scorching our hides. I dropped down the hill, spoke to the foreman, and we assembled the crew as quickly as possible. It was out of the question to get back up the mountain to the fire camp. Our best chance to get out was down Castle Creek about two miles to the river. There was no trail down the creek and I knew the going would be slow along the brushy log-choked creek bottom. I decided to abandon the tools in order to make better speed, as there was serious danger that the fire would spread downstream along the slope fast enough to cut us off. The men strung out down the creek, with the foreman in the lead. I brought up the rear to make sure there were no stragglers. The men were nervous, but fully under control.

The smoke was so dense nothing much could be seen, but we could hear the muffled roar and crackle of the fire and the crash of falling trees along the slope to our right. An occasional swirl of the high wind parted the smoke so that the flames could be seen sweeping wildly through the heavy stand of dead timber. For a time the fire moved downstream faster than we were traveling, but the head of the fire kept to the slope and it lagged enough in the creek bottom so that we kept ahead of it. The men were laboring and cursing as they wallowed through the thick brush and clambered over and under the great downed logs that choked the creek. At length we left the fire behind and came out on the river trail, and so back to the fire camp at the mouth of Bald Mountain Creek.

The next morning, August 14, I took the crew back to Castle Butte, a climb of 4,500 feet above the river. Reinforcements of twenty-five men had come in, so we were forty-five men strong at the upper camp. Townsend took charge of the crew and undertook to cut the fire off below the lookout while I scouted. The fire was burning hard in Castle Creek Canyon where it had driven us out the day before, and in the late afternoon, to my dismay, it crossed the river.

On the 15th there was a tremendous smoke up the river, and it was obvious that the fire had gotten quite beyond possibility of control for some time. Supervisor Wolff scouted east on the Lolo Trail and tried to get down the Eagle Mountain Trail to the river, but the fire had already passed that point and drove him back.

The Missoula district office now got into the game and commenced moving in men and pack stock. They arranged for the Clearwater Forest to move men in on the Lolo Trail and for the Lolo Forest to bring a crew down from Powell Ranger Station to try to cut off the march of the fire up the Lochsa Canyon. By the 17th we had the fire line pretty well completed on Bald Mountain Creek and there seemed nothing to do but follow the fire up from the rear, cutting it off along the flanks. Flint flew over the camp in the fire patrol plane and dropped a map of the fire and the morning paper from Spokane. The fire was up the river as far as Weir Creek, and Ranger Ed Mackay was moving down with fifty-two men. I sat late at night alone on the lookout and watched the fire—a thrilling sight. Castle Creek and Buck Creek below me were lighted up like a city at night, with dead snags still burning while the live edge of the fire was defined in wavering loops of light. Across the river the fire edge rose in a straight breast out of the canyon, and at the top, outlined in fire, was the image of a gigantic bear's head snarling down the river, with long fangs of flame—a most impressive symbol. I felt much depressed, and hopeless of accomplishing much.

The following day I moved in a new camp to a spring just off the Lolo Trail two miles east of Castle Butte, and Townsend took the crew of forty men down the Eagle Creek Trail to try and cut off the fire on Lost Creek. The fire moved up so fast he lost what little line he could get in. He fired a foreman and fifteen men because they would not stand up to the fire. I spent the night in Townsend's camp. We were camped at a spring on the hillside, just under the summit. The airplane dropped another map for us. They circled, then swooped low, dropped the message carrier, and zoomed over the ridge, barely missing the treetops.

I went out with the crew next morning. We started in the creek bottom in Lost Creek and by noon had successfully carried the line out to the ridge top. This line held, and the next day we attacked the fire on Buck Creek. More men were coming in all the time, and Assistant Supervisor Gerrard of the Clearwater had come up. The Old Man fire across the river was smoking up big, and Ashpile Creek up the river went out with a great mushroom of smoke. I knew Mackay must be having trouble upriver.

On the 21st I got word over the telephone from District Forester Kelley that he wanted me to take charge of the entire fire and coordinate the efforts of all three Forest Service organizations working on it. The plan was for the Clearwater to carry the line eastward along the Lolo Trail. The Selway had succeeded in cutting off the fire in the canyon on the downriver side, and the crews were moving forward on the south side while the Lolo men were vainly battling with the run of the fire up the river.

I turned over command of operations on the north side to Gerrard and rode out along the Lolo Trail to Indian Post Lookout, passing the heads of Lost Creek, Indian Grave Creek, Weir Creek, and Post Office Creek. They were all afire halfway up from the river, and it looked like dangerous business to put camps down into them above the fire. It was a relief to get away from direct contact with the fire for a day, and I enjoyed that ride along the high divide in the cool of the morning. Three big bucks with horns like rocking chairs got up before me and bounded away with the distinctive high-jumping run of the blacktail.

Along the Lolo Trail I met Cool from the district office escorting three strings of Montana cayuses loaded with supplies and equipment. He had been four days en route from Powell Ranger Station and had crippled and abandoned two horses along the trail. The half-broken cayuses with sawbuck saddles were quite a contrast to the sleek mules of the government pack strings, well and uniformly equipped with Decker saddles and capable of carrying 250 pounds per mule.

I spent the night at Indian Post Office, a most remote spot in the Clearwater wilderness. It was near this summit that the Lewis and Clark journal comments, "From this elevated spot we have a commanding view of the surrounding mountains, which so completely enclose on us that though we have once passed them, we almost despair of ever escaping from them without the assistance of the Indians."

On the 22nd I rode from Indian Post Office down the Squaw Creek Trail to the river, and made contact with the Lolo forces under Supervisor Simpson. Simpson and Ranger Ed Mackay had been fighting a losing battle since the 18th. The fire was making tremendous runs up the Lochsa River Canyon every afternoon, going over their puny fire lines as though they did not exist. Three times, once in the middle of the night, they had been obliged to dump their camps in the river and retreat in some confusion to save their lives. The march of the conflagration up the canyon seemed irresistible and almost hopeless to check.

When I arrived, reinforcements and more overhead and equipment had come in from Missoula to back up the more-or-less demoralized and discouraged men who had been retreating before the fire. The crew, 150 men strong, was at what we called the beach camp, a wide rocky bar on the edge of the river four miles below the Jerry Johnson Cabin, which had been selected as the safest possible place in the face of the fire. I arrived just at supper time and found long lines of men filing past the extemporized tables where the cooks were dishing out huge helpings of meat, potatoes, beans, and coffee. After supper we held a council of war of all the Forest Service officers assembled in camp. Besides Simpson and Mackay, there were Thieme, Lommasson, and Sandvig from the district office, Rush from the Absaroka, and Ranger Olsen, who had come all the way from one of the Utah forests to help out. They were all experienced fire fighters and men to depend on.

All sorts of suggestions had been made to stop the inexorable move of the fire up the river, from rigging up relays of pumps to building wide fire lines a mile or two in advance and back firing. Our final decision was to get in as close to the fire as possible early in the morning and try to push the fire line both ways from the river. If we got a favorable day or two we could crowd the fire up out of the draft of the canyon. If bad weather continued we could expect to lose our lines and fall back once more.

We were short of beds that night, and the best I could find was a spare canvas fly to roll up in. I was at any rate glad to get back to the river, where I could get a decent wash. I had been on the fire for fourteen days with no baggage save a towel and a pair of socks, and was indescribably filthy with the dust and sweat of the fire line. A fire camp is no place for a fastidious man. One learns to gladly tuck under one's chin the dubious blankets a half a dozen fire fighters may have slept in, to drink out of a common cup or water bag with fifty men on the fire line, and to let the flunkies slop great dippersfull of food onto a tin plate with more than a suspicion of grease on it and devour it with appetite.

The cook's breakfast call got us out in the dark of the early morning, and the first gray of dawn saw us out of camp. Simpson, Sandvig, and Olsen took half the crew down to Post Office Creek on the north side, while Thieme, Lommasson and Rush, with their crew, waded the river and started a fire line up a steep slope through a thick jungle of young timber on a ridge overlooking Colgate Creek. It was a desperate place to attack the fire if the weather turned at all bad, and I must confess I had little hope of the attack succeeding unless the conditions changed for the better.

After getting the crews started I went into camp to get on the telephone. One of the packers reported seeing a spot fire near the Jerry Johnson Trail on the east side of Post Office Creek. If this were true we had a fire east of our lines, and plans would have to be changed radically. I mounted my saddle horse and started up the trail to reconnoiter. By the middle of the afternoon I had satisfied myself that it was a false alarm and rode back down to the river. At the Jerry Johnson Cabin I stopped for a moment and found Ed Mackay with a new group of twenty-five men who had just come down from the Powell Ranger Station and three pack strings loaded with tools and supplies. I was anxious about conditions at the beach camp and rode on down the river in that direction. A mile above camp was what is known as the Colgate Lick, one of the biggest game licks in the country. It is, or was, an interesting spot; a saline spring located in a grove of gigantic cedars. Elk trails converge from all directions, and over an area of three or four acres the forest floor under the cedars was bare as a stock corral from the tramping of herds of game.

Half a mile from the lick I met two scared fire fighters running up the trail. They told me I couldn't get through, that the fire had spotted in below the trail near the elk lick and was burning furiously. This looked bad. It meant that the beach camp was cut off from any possible retreat and might be in considerable danger. I determined to get through if possible, and sent my horse back to the Jerry Johnson Cabin with instructions for Mackay to hold the men and the pack strings there. I hurried down the trail and could soon see smoke and hear the crackle of flames ahead of me. Two cow elk dashed by me. I encountered the fire a quarter of a mile before getting into the lick. It was still below the trail and I hoped yet to get through. I broke into a run, and as I came into the lick there was a tremendous burst of flame ahead of me in a dense thicket of young cedar and white fir, with the terrifying rushing sound of fire crowning through green timber. It was hopeless to get through, and I turned and dashed back the way I had come. The fire was coming up the hill fast and burning so close to the trail that it was only by a close shave that I managed to get by at top speed.

There was nothing for it but to return to the Jerry Johnson Cabin and hope for the best. Mackay had established a camp there, and supper was under way for the men. The smoke from downriver rolled in. The sky was a ghastly yellow and by seven o'clock it was pitch dark. We were by no means sure that our position would be tenable, and at eight o'clock Mackay started the pack strings, which had been kept saddled and waiting, back up the river. We got out a supply of lanterns and had them ready for a night retreat if necessary. The men all rolled into their blankets, and Mackay and I lay down on the bunks in the cabin with our clothes and boots on, leaving the smoke chaser there to keep watch. At ten o'clock he reported the fire in sight. We got little sleep that night. The fire came within a quarter of a mile of us on the north side—the side we were on—and swept clear past us on the south side. Through the dense cover of smoke we could see ridge after ridge flare up across the river, and a spot started close to the riverbank half a mile above the cabin. Several times I was about to rouse the men and move out. Mackay was a reassuring presence, and he felt we could safely stick it out. If we did get cut off we could always take to the river. About one o'clock in the morning the wind died down and the run of the fire ceased.

At the gray of dawn in the morning I was off down the trail for the beach camp, leaving Ed Mackay with his twenty-five men to do what he could with the most dangerous spot fires along the river. A half mile below the Jerry Johnson Cabin I ran into the edge of the fire. Getting through on the trail seemed out of the question, so I dropped down to the river and made my way along the beach to the camp, where I got the history of the preceding day from Simpson and Thieme. The fire had spotted over from the Colgate Ridge inside of Thieme's line and set fire across the river just below the Colgate Lick. Thieme withdrew part of his men to try to get to these spots, and about the middle of the afternoon everything broke loose at once. The fire swept clear over Thieme's line, and Simpson lost everything on Post Office Creek. The Colgate Lick fire cut them off from retreating up the river, but fortunately the main fire on the north side did not advance that far, and while the fire burned to the water's edge just across from camp, the beach camp itself was safe, though they spent a pretty anxious night.

Evidently another retreat was in order, but it was impossible to get a pack string through the fire on the trail to get out the outfit, so the kitchen outfit and supplies were temporarily abandoned on the beach and each fire fighter took a bedroll and one tool and made his way upriver to the Jerry Johnson Cabin, which was to be our next base of attack. The whole outfit was pretty well disorganized, and one detachment which had been working on Post Office Creek had not been able to get to the beach camp the preceding night. We were somewhat worried about them, but they straggled in about noon.

We now had 160 men at the fire camp. The fire had run so far that we hardly knew where to start a new attack until we had done some scouting. One crew picked up the most advanced spots along the river while the other cleared the Jerry Johnson Trail for a backfire to be used if necessary. Fortunately, as often happens after a big run, the fire lay rather quiet that day. In the afternoon I scouted up Warm Springs Creek, which comes into the river from the south two miles above Jerry Johnson. There is a splendid big hot spring which pours into the creek, and a big lick, even bigger than the Colgate Lick. I surprised two elk and three blacktail deer in it as I walked up the trail. As near as I could tell in the dense smoke, the fire had not gotten into Warm Springs Creek, but stopped in the ridge to the west.

That night at a council of war, we decided that in the hopes of a better break in the weather conditions, we would try the same tactics again and start new lines on both sides from the river close to the fire rather than to try backfiring. I got encouraging reports over the phone from the Clearwater and Selway. Paul Gerrard was making great headway along the Lolo Trail, moving his camps forward across one drainage after another, and had already reached the West Fork of Post Office Creek. The Selway had one twenty-five-man crew at Gold Meadows and one at Flytrap Butte, and these crews were gradually moving their lines forward along the north side. We had a few drops of rain at night, which would hold the fire from running much for a day or two.

From the 26th to September 1, in spite of many setbacks, we were successful in driving the fire lines pretty well back from the river, and felt that we had checked the main run of the fire. There was still an unburned strip of a mile between the Colgate Springs fire and the main fire on the north side, so we moved crews back to the beach camp and the Post Office camp. On the first we had a man killed. I had just been over a hot sector of the line we were having difficulty in holding, as it was a steep slope below the fire, and big rocks loosened by the fire were rolling down across the line and snags were dropping frequently. Two brothers were working with a saw on the line when a tall snag came down without warning. It caught one of the men before he could move, crushing his skull and killing him instantly. There is always a considerable element of danger on the fire line. In my own experience I have seen three men killed in this manner, and narrow escapes are frequent. Minor accidents such as axe cuts, broken limbs, and sprains occur regularly.

On the eighth of September fire lines were connected with both the Clearwater and Selway crews, and the fire was under control. As near as I could figure, there were about ninety-five miles of held fire line. The fire fighting forces at the end of the job totaled 480 men. After thirty-three days in fire camp I was indeed glad to take the trail to Powell Ranger Station and a car into Missoula. A soft bed and a civilized meal with a white tablecloth seemed to me the most desirable things in the world.

CHAPTER 6

The Moose Creek Story

Old Bob Monroe threw a couple of chunks on the campfire, which had been allowed to burn down to a bed of coals, as all good cooking fires do. The sparks flew high in the gathering dusk, and in a minute or two the flames burned up brightly, illuminating a circle in the camp on the edge of a mountain meadow.

The camp was snugged down for the night. Tom Grant, the Nez Perce Indian packer, had stacked his packsaddles one on top of the other, covering the pile with a manta, and tied it down securely with a cargo rope so there would be no wet rigging in the morning. Supper had been cooked and eaten, and the dishes washed and stacked upside down with the frying pan on top and a tarp thrown over them to keep off the night dew. Each man had spread his bed in what he hoped was a soft spot under a spruce tree. From outside the circle of the fire across the meadow came the soft crop of the horses and pack mules filling up on the sweet grass after a long day on the trail. Occasionally came the jangle of the bell on the white bell mare.

The boys had just cleaned up on a stubborn five-hundred-acre fire in the Old Man Creek Canyon. The fire was all out, burning snags felled, and mop up of the edges completed. The fire fighters had gone out yesterday, and the little party of rangers and guards remained to pack out the balance of the camp in the morning.

The men gathered around the now brilliantly blazing fire, ready for an hour's relaxation before bedtime. Old Bob squatted on one heel by the fire in a position he could maintain without apparent discomfort all evening. He pulled a lighted brand from the fire and applied it to his filled pipe.

"Better look out, Bob," said one of the men jocularly, "You will burn up the rest of that red beard of yours that you saved from the fire last Monday. When I saw you come out of that last run of the fire behind the crew, pushing that fellow Whitey ahead of you, I couldn't tell which was sparks and which was that beard of yours shining."

"Would have been all right," grunted Bob, "if Whitey hadn't gotten stampeded. I admit it was pretty tight for a little while when that run of fire started up the hill, but I had the men all lined up to make their get-away when that Whitey started crying and praying and saying we was all going to die. I had to be real rough with him; batted him over the ears and booted him ahead of me, and we came up through the smoke a fogging."

Bob Monroe was the district ranger and had fought fire for nearly forty years through all the Clearwater country from the Salmon to the Lochsa, and everybody knew he was the man to do the right thing in a tight spot. He was as old in the Forest Service as the Service itself was.

"Funny how different fellers acts in a fire when things look bad."

This was from Jim Girard, the veteran timber cruiser, who for years had been called off his timber job whenever a really bad fire situation developed. Jim rolled a cigarette and continued.

"Some of them keep their heads and some of them go plumb crazy when a fire gets acting up too bad. You never can tell what a man will do till you have tried him out."

I pricked up my ears then, for I knew a lot of stories about Jim.

"Sure Jim," I said maliciously, "Tell 'em about the time you wrote your will."

Everybody laughed, and Jim just grinned. They all knew that story, how Jim, scouting alone in the big Clearwater Canyon fire of 1919, had got caught in the surge of the fire up through the canyon and had weathered it alone beneath a rock ledge up to his nose in the river, while the fire sucked up the chute of the canyon, burning the very moss off the rocks in the edge of the water. When things cooled off a couple of days later, Jim showed up in camp, where they had given him up for dead, and later somewhat shamefacedly admitted that when things looked toughest he had remembered that he had never written a will, and so scratched his final will and testament on a smooth piece of shale rock and propped it up on a ledge, hoping that some fisherman might discover it in the case his burned body was washed down the river. So far as anybody knows, his holograph will still reposes on the rock ledge in the canyon.

The talk became general. There are two surefire things to get a bunch of Forest Service men to reminiscing around a campfire. One of them is bear stories, and the other is forest fires.

Two young smoke chasers, forest school boys from the University of Idaho, were sitting on the far side of the fire taking it all in, but not saying much. Finally one of them remarked, "Things must have been plenty different when you didn't have any smoke jumpers to parachute to a fire, or any airplanes to drop supplies where you want them."

Old Ed Thenon broke in then. He was the oldest man in the group, older even than Bob Monroe, and had been a ranger on the Clearwater Forest as far back as 1906. He was a dour sort of an old chap, and it was only rarely one could get him started reminiscing.

"Sure it was different," he said. "We not only didn't have no smoke jumpers and no airplanes, we had no roads and damn few trails. We didn't have no remount station to send us an organized pack string, and no central warehouse to ship us an outfit ready to go on a fire. Time we got an outfit together, and hired a pack string, and picked up a crew, and walked them in maybe seventy-five miles to a fire, it was sometimes a week or ten days before we could get a crew on a fire. And the men we had to fight fire with in 1910! Boy, oh boy, it was more trouble fighting the men in those days than to fight the fire! They was always drunk when we hired them, and time and again they used to walk out on us just when we needed them most, and you never could tell what they would do when the fire got going bad and the flames going up through the trees with a whoosh. There's a heap of difference in men. Some of them is real men like you fellers are that can use their heads, but there's a lot of them driftin' around the country that's just like cattle, that's all they are—a mouth and a belly, but no brains—just cattle."

"Where were you in the big Idaho fire in 1910, Ed?" I asked. "I have heard some yarns about a little difficulty you got into back in the Moose Creek country somewhere."

Ed had been standing up warming his backside by the fire. With the conservatism of an old frontiersman, he could never be induced to wear the standard Forest Service uniform. He was dressed in a pair of trousers that somewhere near approximated the uniform, a blue work shirt, and a disreputable hat which bore a faint resemblance to the Forest Service uniform headgear. Deliberately he rolled up a short chunk of log and seated himself comfortably, and got his pipe going good.

"We had quite a time that year. 'Long about the first of August Major Fenn,[1] the forest supervisor down at Kooskia, told me he wanted me to take Charlie Werner and John Olsen with me and survey out some ranger stations back on the Bitterroot Range, between Montana and Idaho. We got our outfit together, a saddle horse apiece and two packs and about a week's grub, and off we went up the Selway River. It was a day to Pete King, and a day to Dry Bar, and another day to the Three Forks Ranger Station. From there on there wasn't no trail except elk trails, but we made it up a burnt ridge and camped on a nice little lake just under the summit. There was good grass there and wood, so we surveyed out a ranger station, and set the corners all proper. Our next job was over in Packer Meadows at the head of the Lochsa. It wasn't more than thirty miles through the mountains, but there wasn't no trail, that way, so we had to go way down Lost Horse Creek to the Bitterroot Valley and then up the valley till we came to the town of Lolo. We got some more grub there, and moseyed along up the Lolo Trail to some hot springs about twenty-five miles up the creek.

"We was just pulling in to camp when along comes a feller with a team and buckboard. He asked if I was Ed Thenon, and I told him he had the right man. He said his name was Greeley, the district forester down in Missoula. I hadn't never seen him, but of course I knowed who he was, and he was a fine man. He said Major Fenn had wired him that the last lightning storm had started ten or twelve fires, and three of them had blowed up, and Fenn wanted me to come back and take charge of a crew of men. Greeley said he had started a crew of forty-five men from Darby with a pack string up Lost Horse Creek, and I was to overtake them and take charge of them on the fire.

"I hadn't lost no fires, but orders were orders, so early next morning Charlie and John and I made tracks back down the creek to Lolo. Greeley had arranged for a boxcar to ship our stock to Hamilton on the railroad. So we loaded the horses and outfit in the car and got off on the local freight that evening to Hamilton.

"The fire crew had about three days' start on us, so we moseyed along as fast as we could on a mighty rough trail. The second day out we met about fifteen fire fighters coming down the trail. They said they had enough fire fighting already, so they just ditched their tools and left. That's the way men was that year, you couldn't depend on them at all.

"That night we caught up with the pack train, camped just over the summit at the lake where we had surveyed the ranger station. We was still a day's travel from the fire. I didn't know the packer. He was a feller from the Bitterroot Valley, a pretty good man, but he had a string of ornery half-broke Montana cayuses, and had been having a lot of trouble along the trail. I had a chance to size up the crew that night. There was five lumberjacks, good men with good woods clothes and corked boots. Then there was seven or eight kids—punks I call them—with caps on and hands in their pockets all the time, the kind you see around poolrooms and cigar stores. The rest of them was about an average crew of fire fighters, drifting workers picked off the freight trains and off of Front Street. They wasn't so hot, but with fifteen of the worst of them already gone out, I thought I could make them do. At any rate they had the whiskey pretty well out of them after four days on the trail.

"The cook was a big fat feller, named Gus Johnson. He hadn't been out on fires before, but was a pretty good campfire cook, and his grub was all right.

"We made Three Forks Ranger Station next day about noon, and there I met ranger Louis Fitting, who was to take us in to the fire about eight miles up Moose Creek. I had been up that way before, and knew there wasn't no horse feed near the creek, so Charlie and John and I left our horses in a meadow behind the ranger station. Louis Fitting was coming back the next day, so he took his saddle and packhorse with him.

"Louie and I left the station ahead of the pack string so we could pick a place to camp. He showed me the fire, which had come over from the next creek to the west, and had burned about halfway down the side of the mountain. It was burning pretty good, crackling and roaring behind the smoke, and once in a while I could hear a big spruce crown out. I didn't like the looks of it no way, so I decided we would camp down on Moose Creek about a mile from the fire till I had a chance to do some scouting and see what kind of a fire I had picked.

"We was just in time to head off the outfit, and we cut a shoofly trail down through the brush to the creek. The air was so smoky you couldn't see more than a few yards, but I picked a place in a big cedar flat. The trees was five or six feet through, and so dense you could scarcely see the sky.

"The cook dug a pit and built a fire, and I set all hands to making camp. I put up my little tent, which was the only tent in the outfit except a fly to put over the cook's grub.

"As soon as the packer got his loads off, he says: 'I am going to get out of here right away with my outfit. I sure don't like the looks of this place at all.'

"I thought he was plumb right, and as quick as he could get his mantas and ropes cargoed up he swung on his lead horse and off he went down the trail. Louie Fitting had left his horses at a little slough about a mile and a half down the trail, and now he said he was going to get them and bring them to camp so he would have them ready to get out first thing in the morning. I said I would go along with him. When we got out of the big cedars and up on the trail there was a kind of a ghastly yellow light over everything. Louie said he had never seen anything like that and neither had I.

"When we got the horses and started back for camp it got so dark we couldn't hardly see the trail. I struck a match and looked at my watch, and it was only four o'clock. I said my watch must have stopped, and Louie looked at his and said, no, his was just the same. When we got opposite the camp we couldn't see nothing at all, and I hollered for someone to come out with a palouser and light us in to camp. Finally Charlie came over with a light, and we pulled down into the creek to camp. It was dark as pitch, but they had a fire going and some candles lighted. The cook called us to supper, and then seeing as there was nothing else to do we all went to bed. I couldn't sleep, and pretty soon I heard a patter on the tent roof, and thinking it might be rain I got up to look. The wind was coming up and moaning through the treetops, and the needles and trash was dropping down on the tent. I says to myself, 'Damn, why couldn't it just as well be rain?' and went and lay down again.

"Pretty soon Louie Fitting called, 'Ed?' I says, 'What's the matter?' and Louie says, 'Come out here, I just saw a star fall on the hillside across the creek, and it has started a fire.'

"I was outside right away, and sure enough there was a small fire starting on the mountain opposite our camp. I knowed well enough that no star could fall and start a fire, so I looked around in the west were the wind was coming from, and the whole sky was pink. I knowed at once all about Fitting's star and where it come from.

"The fire was coming on fast; already it was beginning to throw shadows in the camp, and we could hear a rumble like a railroad train crossing a bridge. I roused the men up and run out into the creek to see what our chances were. The creek was about eight inches deep on the riffles, and maybe twenty feet wide. There was a sandbar on our side and a steep rock ledge on the far side. Just below the sandbar there was a hole maybe a foot and a half deep. There was a big drift pile of logs and trash at the upper end of the sandbar.

"The men was all up by now and they was pretty scared. Some of them were beginning to cry and take on, but there were a few of them just as cool and calm as ever, and they were the ones that helped to save our lives that night. Of course I knew I could depend on Charlie and John and Louie, and maybe the five lumberjacks. The rest of them was just like sheep. I was pretty scared myself, and I could feel my stomach begin to tighten up when I saw how the glare and roar were increasing and getting nearer.

"I hadn't been with the crew long enough so they really knew who was boss; it takes a little time before a crew of men find out. I ordered the men to move all the grub and camp outfit out onto the sandbar and put it in one pile. Some of them were so excited and scared they wanted to start running down the trail ahead of the fire. I got up on a log and says to them, 'Men, if you leave here you will be burned up sure. We have got to all stay together here and lay down in the creek and cover our heads with blankets when the fire goes over, and we will come out of it all right.'

"The cooler hands got busy moving our outfit over on the sandbar, while I was sizing up that drift trying to decide whether to set it on fire and burn it up before the crown fire reached us, or to try to keep it from burning till the overhead fire had passed over us. I did not want the drift pile and the crown fire over our heads to burn at the same time. I got a water bucket and decided to try to keep the drift from burning till the overhead fire had passed. The men were busy piling up our camp outfit on the sandbar. The fire was getting closer all the time and burning bark and big chunks of fire were raining down on us all the time. The drift had caught fire several times and been put out with water, and so had the canvas over the grub pile on the bar.

"Charlie and Louie got the two horses into the deepest part of the creek and covered them over, heads and all, with wet blankets. It was light as day now in the camp, and the timber on the mountains on both sides of the creek was all afire. Trees were crashing down all around us, and the sight and sound of the fire was something terrible. The smoke lifted a little on the west side of the creek, and here, halfway up the mountain, was a whirlwind of fire just like a waterspout only it was all fire and burning gas and a thousand feet high. It moved back and forth

and up and down the slope, and the roar of it was like a million blow-
torches. If it had ever moved down on us we would have gone out just
like when you touch a candle flame to a mosquito. I was most too busy
throwing water to look, but I heard a commotion among the men, and
two of them had gone plum crazy. One of them was old Gus, the cook,
and the other was a little German named Heinrich. Three of the men was
trying to hold Gus down in the water, and Heinrich was dancing around,
singing lullabies and praying. I told John and one of the lumberjacks to
throw Heinrich into the deepest water and put a blanket over his head
and hold him down. The three other men had got the cook down in the
water and sat on him. Some of the other men were pretty wild, but the
cooler heads were taking care of them, and they were all laying down in
the creek with blankets over their heads.

"I looked down the sandbar and saw that all the men was in the
creek except Charlie and Louie Fitting. They were throwing water on
the blankets over the horses. I saw some white things floating down the
creek and then I could see they were trout, floating belly up. I thought,
'My God, if the water up the creek is hot enough to kill the fish what
will we do when that comes?' I didn't have long to think about it. The
grub pile and the drift pile was both burning. I grabbed my bucket
and threw a splash of water on the canvas, and just then the crown fire
came directly over us, and a wave of heat struck right down on me, and
I staggered around and dropped to my knees. I thought then that this
was it, and my time had come, but as I dropped to my knees I put the
bucket over my head, and that cut off the heat till I could get a breath,
and I fell into the water with the bucket still over my head. I didn't have
no blanket, and the bucket sure saved my life.

"I lay there about ten minutes. I guess I wasn't more than about half
all there. Finally I raised up and looked around a bit. The worst of the
crown fire had passed over us, though everything around us was still
burning. The crazy Dutchman was still singing under his blanket and
now and then calling for someone to throw a bucket of water over him.
Nobody was moving except Charlie, who was throwing a bucket of water
on the horse blankets and then laying down again.

"Pretty soon the men commenced crawling out of the creek onto the sandbar, and huddling around the heap of coals left by the burning drift to dry out their clothes. The snags and blazing dead trees across the creek gave us plenty of light to see. The grub pile and canvas were a heap of ashes. Three of the men and I had got so smoked up we could hardly see, and the pain in our eyes was terrible. Nobody was burned very bad, except a few of the men had got the backs of their hands blistered holding the blankets over their heads.

"There was still considerable danger from falling timber. One big cedar snag came down right across the creek. Somebody yelled 'Look out,' and two of the men who were right in line with it dived under the bank. We all thought they was gone, but when the cloud of ashes went down they crawled out, looking scared and kind of foolish. Then Charlie went down to the creek and picked up a bucket, and just when he bent over and reached for it a snag dropped and smashed the bucket flat. If the bucket had been a foot further away Charlie's head would have been the same way.

"The horses had stayed very quiet all through the fire with the blankets over their heads. They weren't really burned at all, except the hair was scalded off their rumps in one or two places where the fire steamed up the water in the blankets.

"By this time it was getting daylight, and we commenced thinking about breakfast. The grub pile was all burned to ashes. John got a chip and started to scrape the ashes off the pile to see if he could find something left. The four of us who had our eyes smoked up were sitting down trying to nurse our eyes, which were paining us like the devil. It was just like being snow-blind, if you ever tried that. One of the lumberjacks said he knew a remedy. He walked over to the grub pile and started digging around, and came back with half a cup of table salt, and told us to dash some in our eyes. I thought it was more ashes than salt at first, but it surely helped us.

"The men now had the grub pile pretty well worked over, but there was nothing left we could eat. Coffee, sugar, flour, bacon, beans—everything was burned up. One of the men took the coffeepot and filled it from the creek and put it on the fire, and said it would look like we was having coffee anyhow. 'Yes,' said another one, 'It ought to be good and stout too with the ashes in the water.'

"Pretty soon Louis, who had been prospecting around camp, said, 'What's the matter with having trout for breakfast?' 'Where are you going to get them?' I says. 'The bottom of that pool is white with them,' says Louie. And sure enough, we fished around and scooped up fifty or sixty big trout, all lying belly up in the water. They hadn't been boiled. The water got good and warm but never did get hot. Anybody that says forest fires boil the water in the creeks is a liar. We cleaned the fish, and as we didn't have no grease to fry them, we put them in a couple of kettles and boiled them, and pretty soon we had a pretty good breakfast.

"There was no reason for us to stay here any longer with no grub and no fires to fight. So far as I knew the whole reserve had burned up clear out to the Bitterroot Valley. I told the men to stay where they were, and Charlie and I would see if we could get through the burn to Three Forks. The whole canyon had burned out, black as your hat. There wasn't a green tree in sight, and logs and snags were still burning here and there. The black ashes were ankle deep everywhere. In most places they had cooled, but wherever a log was still burning they were hot, and we had to be careful not to put a foot down into a pocket of hot coals. By jumping from log to log, and part of the time walking in the creek, we made it down to Three Forks about 3 o'clock. I was afraid the cabin had burned, but the ground around the cabin had been stomped into dust by the ranger's horses and pack stock, so that saved it from burning.

"There was plenty of grub in the cabin, and pretty soon Ranger Adolph Weholt came in with a crew of five or six men. They had been on another fire five miles from us, but had got on fresh-burned ground, and were all safe, but pretty well smoked up. They thought we had all burned up.

"We had a big feed that night, and next morning we took the crew and a couple of packhorses and three crosscut saws and opened the trail up Moose Creek, so we could get back to camp. We got there in the middle of the afternoon, and there was all of the men sitting just where we left them. They was all still kind of dazed, and the funny thing was, they didn't want to leave there. They knew they was safe there, and didn't want to go anyplace else. I finally got them started, and we went back down to Three Forks. The cook had pretty well recovered by that time, but the lullaby boy was still crazy as a coot. When we finally got them out to the Bitterroot Valley they sent him to the asylum in Deer Lodge, and far as I know he is there yet."

Ed got up and stretched himself with his back to the fire.

"Time we was all turning in," he said. "We got a big job packing up this camp tomorrow morning."

In another ten minutes the men were in their blankets, and the camp silent save for the occasional jangle of the white mare's bell across the meadow.

CHAPTER 7

Snowshoes

In winter the wilderness moves down, gradually encroaching on civilization. During the summer months, fifteen miles back from railroad or automobile roads is still on the edge of man's influence. Half a day's easy walk or ride down the trail will take one back. But with below-zero temperatures and four or five feet of snow on the ground, fifteen miles, or even ten miles back is a long way from anywhere. A broken leg or even a broken snowshoe might prove disastrous. Only the grub and blanket pack on the man's back give him food and shelter, and a man is much closer to the primitive life than he is in the same country in summer.

In my early days as forest supervisor, I made many snowshoe trips of three or four days. There was much country to explore, and the summers were all too short to cover all the new country. There was also the advantage that in many rough drainages, with no trails as yet, travel by snowshoes was really easier when the brush and down timber were deeply covered with a blanket of snow. Then too, I was young and vigorous, and the adventure appealed to me.

A few nights lying out in the snow in cold weather is no great hardship to a woodsman. We usually picked a spot where there were convenient standing dead trees, which could be readily felled and cut into logs. Then with a big fire and a green bough bed beside it in the snow, one could spend a fairly comfortable night. In those days the modern down sleeping bags were not available to us, and I usually carried one double wool California blanket, but without the heat of the fire this was entirely inadequate to keep a man warm through a winter night, so frequent replenishment of the fire was necessary, and one expected only broken periods of sleep. It is really more comfortable on a cold night when the snow is dry than at warmer temperatures when everything is wet. I recall one of the most miserable nights I ever spent in the woods. I was out on a three-day cruising trip with Ranger Tom Spaulding and R. Y. Stuart, who afterwards became chief of the Forest Service.[1] Stuart was rather awkward in the woods, and not much used to snowshoes, and Spaulding and I had to occasionally pull him out of the snow when he fell headfirst with his pack into a hole around some spruce tree. The second day out we dropped off a mountain into Little Joe Creek, a rough V-shaped timbered canyon, with no sign of a trail in it. Along in the afternoon a cold rain started, making snowshoeing heavy, and we camped in a little timbered flat along the creek in two feet of snow. As we had no tent of any kind, what we needed was a roaring fire, but Stuart, meaning to be helpful, took the little two-and-a-half pound axe and started to cut down a dead tree. The first thing he did was to break the axe handle off in the eye of the axe. That ended the possibility of getting any good logs for our fire, and we had to content ourselves with such squaw wood[2] as we could pick up, dead limbs broken from trees, and such dry poles as we could break down. The drizzling rain continued all night, and since it was too wet to lie down, we squatted by our inadequate fire through the miserable night, with wet blankets over our shoulders. We were glad to be moving with the first gray of dawn.

Another time—it was January 1908—Karl Woodward and I talked up a snowshoe expedition along the summit of the Bitterroot Mountains from Lolo Pass to Elk Meadows. It was mostly an adventure, though I wanted to study the possibilities of building a trail along the divide, which we did a year or two later. Forest Ranger Thayer met us at Lolo, and thirty miles up Lolo Creek to Hot Springs behind his shaggy team of cayuses was pure pleasure. There was not more than a foot of snow on the road—just enough for good sleighing. That evening we spent at Lolo Hot Springs looking over our packs and making final arrangements. We proposed to take the Lolo Trail to Lolo Pass, then follow the timbered summit of the Bitterroot Range easterly to Elk Meadows, where we would strike an old trail leading down a ridge to the mouth of the South Fork of Lolo Creek. The trip involved less than forty miles, and we were satisfied that we could easily make it in four days, with three nights out.

I had a double California blanket weighing ten pounds which had seen many a campfire up and down the Rockies. Woodward had a pair of army blankets. We carried a very light silk shelter tent, a great addition to comfort when sleeping in the open. Both of us had good web snowshoes. Our food supplies were simple, but just enough for three nights out—bacon, hardtack, rice, erbstwurst, chocolate, raisins, tea, and sugar.

We were off at daylight next morning, making Lolo Pass about noon. Then we began to climb rapidly and for seven hundred feet the snowshoeing was fairly good. As we neared the summit, however, we encountered loose snow, which had absolutely no supporting capacity. Our snowshoes sank to the packed snow beneath, and we had to plough through it. Our progress slowed to about half a mile per hour, and it was middle afternoon when we topped the first summit.

The divide for some distance eastward was a broad ridge, heavily timbered with spruce and lodgepole pine. It was impossible to see any distance. In fact it was impossible to find any of the monuments or blazes which marked the Montana-Idaho boundary on the summit, so deep was the snow. We were left with nothing to guide us but a map and our sense of direction.

We ploughed along slowly through the afternoon, the packs dragging heavily on our shoulders and our legs weary with the constant pull of the snowshoes. The sky was overcast. Foolishly, neither of us had brought a compass, expecting to be guided by the topography of the country. As a result we were confused as to our direction on this first timbered divide.

Finally we became suspicious we were working our way too far to the north and stopped at the first opening in the timber to take our bearings. Our suspicions were well founded. We were on a spur ridge about a mile from the main divide. This mistake fell heavily upon us, and we decided to camp on the spur and retrace our steps the following morning. It was tough enough going so that we sure begrudged the extra two miles. We picked a campsite among a stand of dead lodgepole pines, tramped down as much of the six feet of snow as possible, and shoveled a place for our beds and campfire with our snowshoes. Soon a fire was going, which during the course of the night sank deeper and deeper into the snow. We put up our little silk tent with the open side to the fire so that it would contain and reflect the heat of the fire, and cut a good bed of green fir boughs.

It was intensely cold—nearly 40°F below zero as we afterwards learned from Missoula records—yet we spent a fairly comfortable night, one of us rising about every hour to replenish the fire. When daylight came we were on our snowshoes, retracing our steps back to the main divide.

Again on the divide we continued eastward. On both sides the terrain fell off gradually, with occasional meadows and open glades in the timber. To our left was the Lolo Creek drainage; to our right the immense wilderness of the Clearwater country, at that time hardly more than half explored. As we continued to climb, our snowshoes sank two feet into the powdery snow. By afternoon we dragged heavily. Woodward had a reputation as a cross-country runner at Cornell, and in those days I had a pretty stringy pair of legs myself, but this continual grind was sufficient to exhaust the most hardened athlete. We camped on the ridge just before dark.

I made hard work of getting two dead trees down. In the meantime Woodward had burrowed into the snow and had the fire going and the tent pitched. A little after dark we settled down to a well-earned meal of thick hot erbstwurst soup, bacon, hardtack, and boiled rice with raisins. With our pipes going after supper we began to wonder for the first time whether we were getting into a jackpot that we might have trouble getting out of. We had only one day's food supply left, and we were only halfway to Elk Meadows. It was not too late to turn back, but we decided we would push ahead. That night the cold moderated to zero, and at midnight it began to snow.

In the morning we dug out and swung our packs for another day. The snow continued to fall. The divide gradually made its way up toward Skookum Butte, with an elevation of 7,000 feet. The depth of the snow was incredible; it must have been more than fifteen feet, perhaps twenty-five in places, and in the short alpine growth of spruce and fir we literally walked among the treetops.

There were no small birds or squirrels. Once we heard the dismal croak of a great northern raven, and a single Canada jay had flitted around our last camp. Once when we threw ourselves on the snow to rest for a moment, a mouse fearfully ventured out from a sheltering treetop on the surface of the snow. When he was two feet from his shelter there was a flash of blue, the stabbing of a sharp beak, and a big Steller's jay bore his prey away. We saw one or two marten tracks, but no signs of coyote, lynx, or lion. The four-footed creatures had all left this inhospitable country.

We made only four miles that day, with the most strenuous of efforts, and camped at the edge of a small lake, its waters hidden deep under the all-enveloping snow. We knew it was a lake and not a meadow only by our pocket map. We were beginning to feel the effects of hard travel and broken sleep. We barely had enough food for supper and breakfast. In the morning we took stock of our scanty supply—a small lump of raisins, perhaps two ounces, a cup of sugar in a cloth sack, and a little package of tea. We had to make the climb over Skookum Butte, then one more summit, and we would be on the down trail to the South Fork.

Between gusts of snow we caught glimpses of the timbered saddle ahead and started downhill and, as I was leading, I kept bearing to the left to stay on the crest. We continued in this way for half an hour, making fairly good time, when to our utter discouragement we ran into a fresh snowshoe track. It was obvious what we had done. By continually bearing to the left we had made a half circle around the mountain and were back on our own track. It was bad woodsmanship, but perhaps excusable in view of our exhausted condition and the blinding snowstorm. It was three o'clock before we again made the summit and started down the saddle, this time trying to take a better bearing.

Making camp was a terrible experience. The only dry wood available was a short conical dead spruce eighteen inches in diameter at the top of the snow. My axe blows seemed to have no force, and after every few strokes I would sink to the snow violently nauseated from the exertion and an empty stomach. It was well after dark before we had camp made and a moderate amount of wood in the pile.

By daylight we were on the trail again, but without much punch for the hill ahead of us. It seemed an eternity of effort. I felt as though I had been at it all my life, and had nothing ahead in the future but the drag of one foot after another.

All things have an end, and eventually we dragged ourselves weakly over the summit. The trail blazes were buried many feet in the snow, but our map location seemed sufficiently accurate to insure our taking the correct ridge. While the going was still heavy it was a tremendous relief to get a downgrade in our favor, and to know that we were definitely on the way out of the smothering snow. Three miles down the ridge we made our last camp. For supper we had only hot melted snow water sweetened with the last of our sugar, but it gave us temporary stimulation.

The next day we slowly made our way down the ridge and shortly after noon connected with Thayer, who was waiting for us with his team and sleigh according to appointment. He bore the astonishing news of the culmination of the Ballinger-Pinchot controversy, and the fact that we had a new chief in the Forest Service.[3]

The great wilderness of the Clearwater in Idaho has always had a special appeal to me. Up to twenty years ago, before the period of Forest Service road construction started, it was truly a wilderness. From the St. Joe River on the north for a couple of hundred miles to the Salmon River, and from the summit of the Bitterroot Range for a distance of one hundred miles west to the Nez Perce Prairie, there was not a road or habitation. It was a world of high mountain ranges, timbered ridge after ridge, and deep-cut river canyons, much of it almost unexplored. During the summer the Forest Service had begun to make some progress toward opening up the country with trails and had built a few cabins and lookout stations, but in the winter this vast country reverted to completely primeval wilderness. Not a soul lived in it except a few widely dispersed trappers.

In 1915, for administrative reasons, about 400,000 acres of this Idaho territory on the Upper Lochsa River were transferred to the Lolo Forest and fell under my jurisdiction, since it was considered more readily accessible from the Montana side than from the distant forest headquarters in Kooskia, Idaho. I explored as much of it as I could during the first summer, but I had an overwhelming desire to see what the country looked like in winter, to check up on game conditions, and perhaps mostly, I was moved by the spirit of adventure.

For my companion I selected Ranger Anson B. Hodgins, who is one of the best woodsmen I know. Brought up in the backwoods of Michigan, he had spent most of his life hunting, trapping, and working in the timber. Besides his ability as a woodsman he had a dry humor, an even temper, and was generally one of the best men I knew to tie to on a hard trip. Before we left I got over the grapevine that he had expressed to Frank Hahn a doubt that Koch, right out of the office, could stand up to such a trip as that, and I was determined to show him I could hold up my end.

I had one of the rangers drive us by sled thirty miles up to Lolo Springs, the jumping off place at the end of the road. That evening Hodgins ran across an old pair of skis, and announced he was going to build us a sled. That sounded good to me—anything to take the curse off backpacking—so he spent half the night making a light strong ski-runnered sled. It looked fine. Early in the morning we got off with our packs lashed to the sled. The first half mile was a broken sleigh road, and it went splendidly. Then we had to cut loose from the road and start up the long ridge traversed by the old historic Lolo Trail to Lolo Pass. That was something different. There was a foot of loose snow on top, through which snowshoes and sled had to plow. We settled to the pulling rope and for half a mile pulled our hearts out. We stopped to rest and I looked at Hodgins and he looked at me. Without a word we took the packs off the sled and adjusted them against our backs. We leaned the sled up against a tree, and so far as I know it is there yet.

Snowshoeing was very heavy as the fresh new snow got deeper and deeper as we mounted the ridge. I will confess that I let Hodgins break trail more than his fair half of the way, as he felt so cocky. It was pretty well toward dark when we made the nine miles to the pass and came out on the level white expanse of Packer Meadows. We knew there was a trapper's cabin here and found it, three-quarters buried in the snow. The two brothers, Andy and Carl Erickson, happened to be at home and gave us a warm welcome. The next morning they accompanied us a couple of miles on our way. Andy insisted on carrying my pack and threw the fifty-pound load over one shoulder as though it was a featherweight. He was a moose of a man and strode through the deep snow on his snowshoes with as little effort as any bull moose.

It was all downhill that day, and by the middle of the afternoon we reached the Brushy Cabin, a Forest Service cabin that I had caused to be built that year at the junction of the Brushy and Crooked Forks of the Lochsa River. There was a stove in the cabin and a couple of bunks with a padding of bear grass, so we made ourselves comfortable. As several hours of daylight remained I took a stroll up the course of the Crooked Fork. The stream was frozen or snowed over, except for an occasional hole of open water, and offered excellent traveling. So far we had seen no signs of big game, but as I passed the mouth of a small stream coming in from the west, I could see evidence of a band of elk wintering along it. I swung off the Crooked Fork and up along the side of the side stream, which was spring fed and consequently open water, though it was walled in on either side by buttresses of snow. The elk had worked up and down this narrow open channel, feeding on browse from the bordering willow and alder. Keen with anticipation, I slipped along through the forest, silently on my snowshoes, and then I saw them—a small band of elk, two bulls, still with antlers, three cows, and a couple of calves. When they sighted or scented me they dashed up the channel with a great splattering of ice water and flurry of snow. I followed along the course of the stream and soon sighted them again where they had run into a cul de sac of windfall across the stream. As I approached they stood with their heads turned looking back at me, but reluctant to leave the open channel and plunge into the deep snow. "Poor brutes," I thought. They looked cold and wet standing in the water, with their noses and yellowish coats powdered with snow. I approached within fifty feet. The two bulls turned somewhat belligerently to face me, while the cows and calves crowded into the deep snow on the far side of the channel. I did not think it was wise to disturb them further and retraced my steps, leaving them to their chilly refuge.

The elk which winter in this inhospitable mountain country are probably remnants of the great bands which, prior to the coming of the white man, wintered on the nutritious grasses and in the shelter of the cottonwood bottoms of the Bitterroot and Clark Fork Valleys in Montana, though a considerable part of them probably drifted into the mountains for summer range. Driven off their ranges by settlement, they had apparently adapted themselves to a quite different and more rigorous mode of living.

Hodgins and I were off again in the morning, following down the course of the Lochsa River. In the short distance from the Montana side of the Bitterroot Range to the Idaho drainages, there is a remarkable change in the flora and timber growth, due doubtless to the much greater snowfall of the western side. We passed through forests of giant cedar and towering white pines, which were almost lacking on the Montana side. There was a fairly good trail down the river, but it was deep-covered with snow and hard to follow in places, so we found it was easier and more interesting most of the time to take the frozen and snow-covered river channel. We saw little evidence of big game during the day, but always interesting signs of fur bearers—coyote tracks, marten and mink, snowshoe rabbit, and once or twice the heavy furrow in the snow made by otter between the occasional open spots in the river.

The snowshoeing was fairly good, and we made good progress, but late in the afternoon, as we approached within two or three miles of our destination, the cabin at the Powell Ranger Station, I noticed that

Hodgins began to lag badly, and looking back I could see his face contorted with pain. I stopped till he pulled alongside of me.

"Anything the matter, Hodgins?" I asked.

"Yes," he said glumly. "I've strained those damn cords down the front of my legs and they are giving me hell."

I knew all about that. I had once experienced the same thing myself on an unusually hard trip. It was the dreaded *Mal-de-raquette* of the Canadian voyageurs. When those tendons down the front of the lower leg are strained by the constant drag of the snowshoe in heavy going, the pull of the snowshoes from the toe becomes exquisitely painful, and rest for several days is the only cure. There was nothing for it but to keep on to the cabin. I broke trail, and Hodgins crippled along as best he could, stopping frequently. We made the ranger station shortly before dark. It was a pretty good cabin, set near the river on a wide timbered bar, with a small stream alongside. There were two rooms downstairs and a loft above. The cabin contained a good heating stove and a cookstove, and a couple of rolls of blankets had been left suspended from the rafters to protect them from mice. The two bunks had a good supply of dried bear grass, somewhat mousy and ratty, but it looked as though we could be comfortable. As always, by universal rule, the rangers had left a good supply of wood under cover. Unfortunately no food supplies had been left except for a few odds and ends—half a coffee can of beans, a little coffee, and a moldy strip of bacon hanging from the rafters—so we were dependent on the food we had carried in our packs.

With the snowshoes off, Hodgins was able to cripple around the cabin pretty well, and I was hopeful that a day or two of rest would put him all right. We lay up all the next day except for a few hours' swing I made through the timber in the afternoon. I found signs of moose wintering on a big cedar flat but was not fortunate enough to see them. Our intention had been to make a full day's travel down the river beyond the ranger station, but it seemed evident that Hodgins would not be able to do it. So I decided to snowshoe down the river as far as I could go and yet be back in a day.

I was off at daybreak with a good lunch tied to my belt. The first three miles the river ran evenly through a wide timbered bar, and the water was almost entirely closed over. It was a beautiful morning, and from the open river channel I could see far off on the right the high white divide on which lay the historic Lolo Trail, followed in 1805 by Lewis and Clark, and later by Chief Joseph and his Nez Perce Indians. To my left I caught occasional glimpses of the serried peaks of the main Bitterroot Range touched by the morning sun.

Below the bar the mountains closed in and I entered a narrow canyon, with vertical cliffs or steep mountain slopes confining the river into a series of rapids alternating with bottomless still green pools. Since there was about four feet of snow, there usually was a rim of snow on one bank or other of the river, which afforded good traveling, and frequent snow and ice bridges where one could cross from one side to the other. It was a most fascinating experience to traverse this wild winter canyon, with the river roaring under me, and a little thrill of danger when I crossed a snow bridge and looked down into the dark water, thinking what would happen if the snow gave way.

Once, a pair of otters appeared in one of the open pools, raised their snaky heads out of the water and barked threateningly at me, then dived and disappeared. I commenced to see elk sign where they had crossed the river. It is amazing how boldly they plunge down a four-foot snow embankment into the swift water, and emerge on the other side, doubt-less dripping with ice water. Finally I sighted a band of about fifty elk on the canyon slope above me, about one hundred yards away. They were wintering on the steep south slope where the sun and wind had somewhat reduced the depth of snow, and they were able to get about to feed on the browse the slope afforded. I did not disturb them and they paid little attention to me. They looked in fair condition, but they had three months of winter still ahead of them.

I traveled down through the canyon till well past noon, drawn on by the continually new scenes of snow, rock, and water. I hated to turn back. Below me lay eighty or ninety miles of river canyon, almost unex-plored and entirely uninhabited in winter till one came out at Kooskia. I wanted nothing more than to make the trip all the way through, but it was impossible under conditions as they existed. So reluctantly I turned and retraced my steps up the river. It had been fine all day with the sun shining most of the time and cold enough so the snow was dry, but in the middle of the afternoon it was evident that a sudden change in the weather was imminent. The sky turned gray and the temperature moderated considerably. Before I reached the cabin a drizzly rain commenced to fall. It rained most of the night, but cleared up and turned colder the next morning.

Hodgins tried out his snowshoes, but still could not stand the strain on the tendons in thrusting the snowshoes, though he could walk pretty well. We were getting concerned about the food situation, as our supplies were getting low. We might really have gone hungry if it were not for the beans in the cabin. We cooked up a big kettle of beans with some of the moldy bacon and they formed the *pièce de résistance* of every meal. We had no gun with us so there was no chance of getting game.

The next night was cold and frosty, and in the morning we found a hard crust on the snow that would carry a man without snowshoes. It softened up some during the day, but we decided we could travel at night without the use of snowshoes. Hodgins thought he could make it walking. Fortunately there was a good moon, and we rigged up a palouser with a candle and a tin can with a wire bail. We waited till about nine o'clock in the evening to start, and the crust held up splendidly. It was easier going than on a summer trail, crunching over the hard crust in our rubbers. Walking up the wide white band of the river, with the full moon sailing overhead, and the banks overhung with the mysterious dark border of cedar and spruce forest, was as though we were in a dream world.

We easily made the Brushy Cabin by daylight, and spent the day there, getting off again after dark. Now it was harder going with the climb up to the pass, but the crust held firm, and we still did not need the snowshoes. We reached Packer Meadows just before dawn, and decided to push on to Lolo Springs. The going got a little heavier as we descended the mountain and the morning sun softened the snow, and we were both getting a bit tired. Our packs were not very heavy, as all our grub was gone, but with a double blanket, a mackinaw jacket, and a few cooking utensils and odds and ends we had about twenty-five or thirty pounds, and even that weight dragged heavily on me. When we stopped once to rest I threw off my pack and remarked petulantly that man was never made for a pack animal. Hodgins said without a smile, "Want I should carry it for a while?" I said, "Go to hell," and picked it up and off we went again. We were glad to see Lolo Springs before noon.

One snowshoe trip I made came near being my very last one. Three of my Forest Service friends, Clarence Strong, Pat Thompson, and Bill Rapraeger, had conceived the idea of a winter ascent of Mt. Stuart, north of Missoula, and invited me to go along.[4] I was a bit dubious about it as I was then approaching fifty-nine years, while my friends were all vigorous young men in their early forties, and all of them with reputations as tough men on the trail, but I really wanted to get out. We started before daylight and drove up the Rattlesnake Canyon a few miles to where a switchback trail climbed out of the canyon to the long ridge leading up to Mt. Stuart. I was a bit out of condition, and in the first hour of climbing I was inclined to lag a little behind the others, but as I got warmed up, I began to have that feeling of muscles, heart, lungs, and stomach all working well, and I felt pretty good. Once on top of the ridge the going was easier, and we had several miles of gradual ascent through the timber. We stopped for lunch and built a fire at about the point where the subalpine forest growth of spruce and alpine fir started to replace the lodgepole pine and Douglas-fir of the lower ridge.

With a good lunch and a bottle of beer inside me, I felt so good I commenced to lead out, and got fifty or sixty feet ahead of the others. The ridge we were traveling, which gradually began to be steeper, sloped off easily to our left, but on the right side broke sharply over cliffs into a glacial cirque at the head of one of the Rattlesnake tributaries. Wishing to get a better look into this basin I swung gradually toward the edge. The winter winds had drifted a cornice or comb of snow over the cliff edge. I knew perfectly well the danger of such cornices, and thought I was keeping back a safe distance, but had forgotten that this was only January, and the snow had not yet compacted. Suddenly and silently, without any warning, I felt myself drop straight down, and the next thing

I knew I was hurtling downward, head first, on my back in a smother of snow. A few hundred tons of the cornice had broken off and was carrying me down in a small snow slide. My only sensation was, "This is the finish," and a sort of vague regret that it had to come so soon. I could see rocks and tree stubs flashing by and felt a blow across my forehead. The next I knew I was lying motionless, with a sense of darkness and pressure. I tried to breathe, but the avalanche of loose snow following me had driven so close around my body that it was like being packed in cement; there was no room for even the slightest expansion of my chest. A feeling of panic swept over me, but I tried to collect myself, and thought, "You don't have to expand your chest to breathe; try breathing easily." An inch or two of snow had thawed around my nose and mouth, so I could get a shallow breath into my lungs. I tried again to move, to burst my bonds, but I could not move even a finger or two. Again a feeling of helplessness swept over me, when I suddenly realized that my right hand was free; I could wiggle my fingers, and bend the hand from the wrist. It was evident that my hand projected above the snow, but I could not bend it enough to get to the surface. At least I was not buried deep, and thought, "The boys will be down to dig me out. There is nothing to do till they come." I must have been unconscious for some time after landing, as it seemed only a short time before I could hear and feel something scratching in the snow over me.

When I suddenly disappeared over the cliff, the first thought of my companions was to get down to me. A few hundred yards up the ridge they found a draw extending down into the basin, and at some risk of precipitating another snow slide, they slid down to my rescue. My mittened hand above the snow was the first thing they discovered. The snow was packed tight, but it was dry, and by vigorous scratching with his hands and shoveling with a snowshoe, Rapraeger got me uncovered and heaved me out of my snowy grave. A cut across the bridge of my nose had been bleeding profusely, and my face was covered with blood, but I managed to stand upright, my snowshoes still on my feet. I was still in a sort of daze, and tried to straighten up when a shot of pain through my side doubled me up. "I think my back and side are hurt, and I can't see,"

I gasped. Apparently the pressure of the cold snow against my eyeballs had in some way temporarily paralyzed the optic nerve, and I could see only a blur. Rapraeger helped me to move a few feet, and I felt myself gradually coming to. In the meantime the other men had built a good fire, and Rapraeger led me to it and suggested that I sit down for a while.

"No," I said. "If I ever get down and get stiffened up, I'll never get up again. Let's get going."

There was considerable difficulty in finding a spot where it was possible to get back up on the ridge, but the boys broke trail ahead of me, and I managed to follow slowly. It was a long painful pull down the ridge, and cautiously as I might move, severe twinges of pain in my back occasionally doubled me up. I could still see but little, and had to follow closely behind a leader. It was a relief when the long trek was ended, and I could edge myself onto the car seat and swallow a good shot of whiskey to revive my spirits.

At home the doctor sewed up the cut on the bridge of my nose and found I had a couple of cracked ribs and a badly strained back, but nothing that a few days of rest would not cure. I did not move out of my big easy chair for a week, but really enjoyed it. As the papers had printed somewhat sensational accounts of my accident, practically all my friends came to see me and brought me things to read, and to eat and drink; those afternoon visits, which we got to call "avalanche parties," were a very agreeable termination to my adventure.

CHAPTER 8

Mountain Climbing

I suppose in the course of my life, as a young fellow in Montana, and later as a forest officer, I have climbed several hundred mountains. Many of them were ascended in the course of my work as a forester, to provide a vantage point for mapping or sketching timber types, or to locate or inspect fire lookout stations. A lot of others were climbed just to get on top of them. If I look at a mountain long enough, I just have to see the top of it. I have been on nearly every mountain that can be seen from Bozeman, where I grew up, and from Missoula, where I have spent most of my working life.

Mountain climbing literature has always fascinated me. As a boy I knew Edward Whymper's *Scrambles in the Alps* almost by heart, and I think I read almost everything that has been written on the various assaults that have been made on the great peaks of the Himalayas.[1] My idea of a perfect evening is to be alone in the house, with a good fire in the fireplace, the dog at my feet, a pipe and glass of whiskey at my elbow, and a new book on mountain climbing that will last me until 2 a.m. That is a real evening.

I can make no pretense of being an expert rock climber. The techniques of roping, rappelling, use of pitons, and chopping steps in the ice are all beyond me. Most of the mountains I have climbed in Montana, Idaho, and California have required only good wind and endurance, with perhaps a bit of rock scrambling near the top. It is the high country that I love—the country above timberline, with its struggling alpine tree growth, glacial cirques, mountain meadows with their alpine flowers, melting snowbanks, and finally the breathless moment of surmounting the summit and seeing what lies on the other side.

Of all the mountain country I know I think I like the Beartooth Mountains in Montana the best. It is considerably the highest range in the state, with many peaks exceeding 12,000 feet. Nowhere else have I seen such a vast and continuous area above timberline, with nothing but bare much-glaciated rock, snowfields, glaciers, and half-frozen lakes. Among the interesting and unique features of this country are the grasshopper glaciers. The best known is near the old mining camp of Cooke City, and can be readily reached by horseback parties, but the deposits of grasshoppers in that glacier are by no means as extensive as in another much less well known area in the heart of the high range. I once crossed the range afoot from the Cooke City country to Rock Creek, reaching an elevation of 12,000 feet on the shoulder of Snowbank Mountain. That summer was a warm dry one, and the permanent snowfields and glaciers were unusually contracted. As we approached the summit, the whole country was full of masses of grasshopper remains exposed by the melting snow and ice. The air stank with them, and the streams flowing from the snowfields were entirely undrinkable. There must have been tons of grasshopper debris—legs, wings, and whole bodies buried in the ice and snow or washed out in long windrows along the streams of melting ice. It is assumed that great flights of grasshoppers, locusts they are properly, crossing the range were carried down by a snowstorm and imbedded in the ice and snow. Whether it was a single exceptional occurrence or a periodic one I do not know, but I have never seen or heard of the phenomenon elsewhere.

In the heart of this great mountain mass, Granite Peak thrusts its ugly black granite head to an elevation of 12,842 feet. For many years the mountain remained a virgin peak, though the high country around it was gradually explored and mapped. It was not only the difficulty of the climb itself, but the general inaccessibility of the mountain that protected the peak from assault. It was not possible to attack the mountain from the nearest horse camp, and a backpacking expedition was required, with the additional difficulty of complete lack of fuel wood in the great area above timberline surrounding the peak. However, several unsuccessful attempts had been made. The first known effort was made by the U.S. Geological Survey party in 1889, from the south side, but they were stopped 200 feet below the summit. In 1894 the whole country was explored, and several of the high peaks climbed by a scientific expedition from Seattle under James P. Kimball.[2] They obtained some magnificent photographs of the region, but also failed in their attempt on Granite Peak.

In 1910, and again in 1922, Mr. Fred Inabnit of Billings, a native of Switzerland and an enthusiastic mountain climber, with a small party, made two attempts on the peak, but on both occasions was stopped by unclimbable cliffs. In 1914 two of my Forest Service friends, J. C. Witham and R. T. Ferguson, made a reconnaissance trip and climbed Mt. Tempest and obtained some fine photographs of Granite Peak, but did not actually make an attempt to climb the mountain.

I had always been interested in this mysterious mountain, known as the highest peak in Montana, and had studied all available photographs carefully, especially a very fine view that my brother, Col. Stanley Koch, had taken in 1899 from Mt. Dewey to the south, and which displayed the full east and west profile of the peak. From the study of these photographs I had become convinced that the east ridge, from the Mt. Tempest saddle, afforded the most practicable route of attack. Witham and Ferguson agreed with me, and in 1923 we talked up an official Forest Service expedition to climb the peak. Mr. Fred Inabnit of Billings and a few of his friends and fellow mountaineers had also been planning a new assault on Granite Peak that summer, so it was decided to join forces.[3] The party assembled at the east

Rosebud Lake Chalet on August 26, 1923. Arrangements had been made for a Forest Service packer and three packhorses to accompany us the first day.

We were off early on the 27th for the tremendous climb to the plateau between the forks of Rosebud Creek. This was a three- or four-thousand-foot climb, and it was a very great help to have the pack animals to relieve us of the job of backpacking, though a pretty tough scramble for the loaded horses. About three o'clock we topped out just above timberline on the wide, gently-sloping Rosebud plateau. The traveling was fairly easy up this plateau, a barren, bleak, wide gravely ridge. A few miles farther we got the first view of the top of Granite Peak over the shoulder of Froze to Death Mountain. This south face was distinctly forbidding, the profile of a black, jagged granite ridge, which fell almost vertically

FIG. 21. Granite Peak seen from the north; the Koch party would ascend the ridge to the left.

to the Granite Glacier at its foot. A wisp of a cloud dragged across the summit, making it look even more hostile.

For the night camp we dropped off the plateau into the head of one of the forks of Phantom Creek, where the last stringers of white bark pine pushing up to timberline offered us a supply of wood for our campfire. It was a nice camp: good grass, wood and water, and an imposing view.

From this point we were sending the horses back and loading our pack sacks. Each man carried his blankets and four days' condensed rations, for which we were using the Forest Service smoke chaser rations, each day's supply in a separate cloth sack. As we ascended in the early morning, the plateau narrowed to a rough, rocky ridge, somewhat slower going, but with no particular difficulty. About noon we topped out on Mt. Tempest, which is over 12,000 feet. A deep saddle separates Tempest

FIG. 22. Gnome and Septum Snowfield at the head of Phantom Creek.

and Granite, and we could look across this directly to Granite Peak, not more than a mile and a half away. We were looking squarely at the ridge we hoped to ascend, and it looked jagged and broken, but not unclimbable in our judgment. It seemed too late to make an attempt on the peak that day, so we dropped into the deep saddle and down the side of the mountain to Avalanche Lake, where we proposed to camp at an elevation of 10,400 feet. Since part of the afternoon remained, a few of us undertook a reconnaissance over the Skytop Glacier, which gave us a good view of the southern slope of our mountain. It only confirmed me in the belief that the eastern ridge offered the only possible route to the top. It was a marvelously interesting country of ice, snow, and rock, and I could have well spent a week exploring it and climbing some of the other peaks, but time was limited, and we had to stick to our main objective.

Mountain Climbing

Our camp was on the bare rocky shore of Avalanche Lake. We had expected to camp completely above timberline, and had carried a few packages of canned heat for cooking purposes, but to our surprise found a small clump of alpine fir, an outpost far above the general timberline from which we extracted enough dry branches and twigs for a small cooking fire. Across the lake from our camp a small glacier descended from Skytop Mountain directly into the lake, and through the evening we were entertained by occasional avalanches of ice and rock splashing into the lake waters.

At a council of war after supper, Fred Inabnit still held to his opinion that the southwestern face of the mountain was the most feasible, so it was agreed to separate into two groups, Inabnit and his party proceeding over Skytop Glacier, while Witham, Ferguson, and I reascended to the Mt. Tempest saddle and attacked the eastern ridge.

The night was long and cold. With no warming fire our blankets were quite inadequate to keep us warm and none of us got much sleep.

At daylight the two climbing parties separated, each wishing the other success. Witham, Ferguson, and I had a climb right from the start, up the steep face to the Tempest saddle, which we had descended the night before. A very steep gradient and a succession of rock ledges made climbing slow, but there were no special difficulties in getting back to the saddle. All three of us were in hard condition from the summer's fieldwork, and though at above 11,000 feet we began to feel the elevation with some shortness of breath, we were able to climb at a fair rate of speed.

From the saddle the ridge rose above us at a steep but fairly uniform gradient, covered with loose slide rock of large size, which made climbing slow and laborious. We plodded our way slowly up this slope, and with only a few hand and foot climbs over minor breaks in the ridge, we came out on a small narrow saddle with a cornice of snow in the bottom of it. We were now about 800 feet below the summit, but here is where the real climbing commenced. The ridge above us was very much shattered, with irregular pinnacles, cliffs, and masses of granite. The top of the ridge was clearly unclimbable, with a vertical step rising directly above us. The main north face, to our right, offered little encouragement, as it was an almost perpendicular drop of 1,500 to 2,000 feet to the Granite Glacier below. The only chance was a traverse around the south face. A narrow ledge led to an ugly looking fissure, which seemed possibly climbable. Witham was undoubtedly the best rock climber of the three of us, and I suggested he take the lead. If he could make it I could. Ferguson dropped in behind me. We climbed carefully, hugging the rock closely, and testing each handhold and foothold. There was much loose rock, and constant danger of loosening something to strike the man below. The fissure led us to the top of a spur ridge, from which it was feasible to get back on the main ridge again. A few hundred feet of fair going brought us to another step in the ridge, where a vertical cliff completely barred the way. We stopped for some time to rest and consider. There was only one possibility, an almost vertical chimney, which appeared to lead to a sharp spur ridge on the south face, and would possibly get us nowhere, but at least it led upward, and we decided to attempt it. With Witham in the lead we worked our way up this cleft, with much difficulty and danger. So far as I was concerned this required my maximum ability as a rock climber, and perhaps more than I thought I had. One is upborne by a sort of exhilaration that danger gives, and perhaps this is one of the things that brings men back to difficult climbing. A lost hold here on the part of any of us would have sent a body hurtling down the steep gullies of the south face, with no stop short of Skytop Glacier.

Emerging at the top of the chimney, to our surprise and gratification, a fairly easy route back to the main ridge opened up. But again our route was blocked by another vertical step. This time we could find no break on the south face that seemed possible. We had kept off the north face so far and wanted none of it. But the only chance offered seemed to be a traverse of a narrow upward-trending ledge around this rock face, which dropped vertically 1,500 feet to the glacier. As we filed cat-footed around it, the ledge dwindled to a mere crack in the rocks, made still more precarious by a skift of snow and glaze ice which had swept the summit and remained on this cold north slope. It was the most hazardous part of the climb. It is not so bad when you have both a foothold and a handhold, but when you press your hands and body against the smooth rock face with no hold but the grip of your hobnails on a narrow crack, and out of the tail of your eye you look straight down 1,500 feet, it is not so good. A couple of lines from Kipling ran crazily through my head:

There's a wheel on the Horns o' the Mornin',
an' a wheel on the edge o' the Pit,
And a drop into nothin' beneath you
as straight as a beggar can spit;

Fortunately, the Horns o' the Mornin' held us up, and to our relief the upward trend of the ledge brought us back to the main ridge again. We were now within 100 feet of the summit—a jumbled mass of angular granite boulders and pinnacles. We surmounted several vertical steps by Witham going up over Ferguson's or my shoulders to a point where he could drop us a rope. Overcoming several such obstacles, we triumphantly attained the top—a narrow broken ridge of rugged granite masses, but extensive enough so we could relax and be at ease.

It was 11:10 when we reached the summit, and we remained there for two hours. The view from the peak was extraordinary in scope. Since we were at the highest point in the state, there was nothing we could not look over. To the north almost vertically below us was the Granite Glacier filling a rock-walled cirque; then the eye was carried down the steep canyons of the Rosebud to the open foothills and valley of the Yellowstone River. To the south below us lay the Skytop Glacier, filling the trough between Granite and Skytop Mountains. The fine peaks of Mt. Wilse and Mt. Spofford lay to the west, part of the same ridge as Granite Peak. In the distance, over the Wyoming line, the usually impressive Pilot and Index Peaks seemed dwarfed as we looked down on them. We could see nothing of the Inabnit party, though we afterwards learned they heard our shouts, a few hundred feet below the summit. From what we could see from the summit it appeared almost certain that they had been assaulting an impregnable side of the mountain, and I doubt if there is any other reasonable way to the top other than the path we followed.

Witham had carried a hardwood staff up the mountain, and we

FIG. 23. Elers Koch at the summit of Granite Peak.

proceeded to erect an impressive cairn of loose rock, and from the staff in the top of it we flew an American flag, which we left in place. After eating our lunch there was still the descent to consider, and I confess it made my stomach flutter a bit to think of retracing downward some of the places we had come up. It is always easier, at least on the nerves, to climb with one's eyes fixed on the rock face ahead than to come down, looking into the dizzying depths beneath. We had taken the precaution of piling up several small rock monuments at critical points in the ascent, which proved of great assistance in selecting the same route going down. At a few hundred feet below the summit we sighted the other party filing downward across the glacier, and knew they had turned back unsuccessful.

The weather had been perfect for our climb, but now a thunderstorm was brewing and swept the summit with a ragged flurry of mist and sleet which we were fortunate to escape.

We retraced all the bad places without accident, but when we finally came out in the little saddle with the snow cornice and knew the hazardous part was behind us, we all drew a sigh of relief, and our hearts were filled with exultation. We had done it!

We reached camp at Avalanche Lake at 5:30, where the other party had a welcome pot of hot coffee waiting for us. Our plan was to return to Rosebud Lake by following down Granite Creek, and thence to the East Fork of the Rosebud. Since several hours of daylight remained, and we had used all of the small supply of dry wood in the tiny clump of alpine fir, we concluded to press on down Granite Creek to timberline that evening.

The upper valley of Granite Creek might well have been called "The Valley of Desolation." It was a fairly wide valley, which apparently had been occupied by a glacier in the very distant past, and looked just as the retreating glacier had left it. The entire surface was covered with angular blocks of coarse-grained granite, from the size of a kitchen stove to a small house, with never a sign of vegetation, and it was through and over this rock maze we had to make our way. After the hard day's climb it was the most exhausting work, and there was no letup in the bad going. It was some time after dark when we reached timber and gratefully made camp.

Mountain Climbing

We still had a long hard trek down the East Fork of Rosebud Creek to get back to the Rosebud Lake Chalet. This was a narrow rugged canyon, with a string of small lakes along it, and completely devoid of any trail or track. There was no easy going, just a jumbled mass of slide rock on steep slopes over which we climbed and jumped or crawled, as might be required. Even though our packs were now reduced to fifteen or twenty pounds, the weight and shifting of the pack on one's back continually tended to throw one off balance. I had started this trip with a new pair of Russell pacs, freshly hobnailed with sharp Hungarian nails, but two weeks of constant walking and climbing on the granite rock of the Beartooth country had pretty well worn down my hobnails, and in fact I needed a new pair of soles when I returned to Missoula. The worn nails did not hold well on the granite, which was ice-polished in places, and several times in jumping from rock to rock I had heavy falls which I thought almost broke my ribs. On the whole it was the hardest day's walk I ever experienced. We would have done better to camp en route, as the Inabnit party finally decided to do, but Ferguson was insistent on getting back to the chalet, and we pushed on, and it was well after dark when we stumbled into the hotel, so exhausted after seventeen hours of hard walking we could hardly eat, but triumphant in reporting that we had at last conquered Granite Peak.

This mountain has been climbed only five or six times subsequently. Presumably for an experienced and expert mountain climber it would not be considered a particularly difficult ascent, aside from the difficulty of approaching the mountain, but it still offers a challenge to any mountaineer. One member of a Colorado mountaineer's club who made the ascent reported that he considered it a more difficult climb than the well-known Grand Teton. At any rate it just reached the limit of my own capacity as a rock climber. It seems a small thing, but of all the accomplishments and achievements I may have had in a long life as a forester, the first ascent of Granite Peak is the one that I look back on with the greatest satisfaction. Perhaps it is in doing things that just reach one's maximum limit that gives mountain climbing its appeal. It is well to go all out sometimes.

CHAPTER 9

Growing Trees

From 1921 until my retirement in the spring of 1944, I held the position of assistant regional forester at Missoula, with the title of chief of the Division of Timber Management. During these many years, plus my previous experience in the region, I learned to know the forests and mountains of Montana and northern Idaho intimately. Within the timber-growing zone there is hardly a drainage unit of any significance which I have not seen and traversed—from the lodgepole pine forests of eastern Montana through the ponderosa pine, fir, and larch of western Montana to the magnificent white pine of northern Idaho.

As chief of the Division of Timber Management, my field comprised all of the more strictly forestry activities of the region. This included the cruising, valuation, and sale of timber, timber management plans, tree planting, and the protection of the forests from insects and diseases. Of course the immediate administration of all these activities in the region is handled by the forest supervisors—twenty-one of them. The regional office function is largely inspection, planning, and policies, though all the larger sales of government timber come up for direct action by the regional office.

Growing Trees

The western white pine has always been our most valuable species. Often when white pine stumpage is eagerly in demand at from $5.00 to $6.00 per thousand feet, the associate species—Douglas-fir, larch, white fir, and hemlock—would show a very low or even minus value. Naturally this difficulty of complete utilization complicated the already difficult silviculture of the white pine type, since our objective after harvesting a crop of mature timber is to reproduce as much as possible of the valuable white pine. Much of our activity and study of the forestry problems of the district centered about working out practicable methods of handling the white pine type.

There is no more beautiful forest than a mature white pine stand with the noble gray-ridged clear column of the white pine rising above the vivid green crowns of the associated hemlock and cedar and white fir. The ground cover in such a virgin forest is particularly fascinating and beautiful; along the watercourses and in moister places are fringes of delicate maidenhair fern and great clumps of the tropical-looking sword fern. The smaller plants, refined by the deep shade, are specially interesting. There is the *Clintonia* or queen's cup with its single turquoise blue berry, one of the purest blues in nature, wild ginger with its broad green leaves and aromatic root, gold thread whose roots stripped of bark are of a clear golden yellow, the pale saprophytic dutchman's pipe, and masses and stringers of club moss. The fallen half-rotten logs are often covered with trailing mats of the lovely little *Linnea* or twin flower.

I have spent many days in logging camps, necessary in the course of my work, but I never did like them. Logging, at best, is a ruthless and violent business. The camps are temporary and purely utilitarian, and always a scar in the midst of the forest, leaving apparent destruction behind them. I sometimes go over old timber operations, and while as a forester I may be highly gratified at the success in reestablishing a fine stand of seedling pines, offspring of the seed trees left, still I cannot help recalling what the virgin stand looked like, and knowing that it will be one hundred years or more before we again have a big forest, and of course we never will again grow three- or four-hundred-year-old trees like the ones we have cut down. If we hope to retain any such areas for our future pleasure, they must be specially protected as parks or natural areas. We have a few virgin timber areas set aside in the white pine forests of Idaho, and notable progress has been made in withholding remnants of the noble redwoods of California and the matchless coastal Douglas-fir forest of the Olympic Peninsula. As timber grows scarcer, pressure will inevitably come from industry to log these remnants. Even now the Olympic National Park is under fire. There is much misleading talk about selective logging and the possibility of having our cake and eating it too, but the fact remains that by no forestry measures can a virgin forest of big timber be logged without destroying much of its natural charm.

The lumberjack is a natural product of the hard and tough methods of a logging operation. I have many good friends among lumbermen, but years of work in the big timber do something to a man. The atmosphere of a logging camp is not a cheerful one. A lumberjack is rarely a lighthearted individual, if not morose, and foremen take on pretty much the same characteristics as the men. One hears little of laughter or jokes in a logging camp. The men eat their enormous meals silently, and sit in the bunkhouses or outside them, tired from the heavy work that necessarily goes with the job of manhandling big logs. It is not that the men are worn out by over-hard work, but heavy manual labor day by day seems to affect a man's nature and take some of the joy out of life. Coal miners or metal miners are of the same type.

I often contrast the atmosphere of a logging camp with that of a ranch in the cattle country. Cowboys sing and laugh occasionally and joke with each other; the burden of life sits easily on them. Possibly it is in part due to the difference between living in heavy-timber country and living on the open range. Stump ranchers on their little clearings in Idaho or western Montana have a temperament similar to the lumberjack, quite different from the farmers or ranchers of the valleys and open plains of eastern Montana. The latter are much better company and pleasanter companions. I notice the difference even in our Forest Service rangers. The men in Idaho or western Montana in the heavy-timber country are inclined to be sober and serious like the lumberjack. Their work throws them in contact with the logging operations, and on top of that they have

FIG. 24. Savenac Nursery on the Lolo National Forest.

the mental and physical strain of a three-month fire season every year, which surely tends to sober a man beyond his years. The eastern Montana rangers, who deal more with range management than with timber, take on more the characteristics of the stockmen. When one attends one of their ranger meetings there is far more lighthearted laughter and banter between men than in a similar group of Idaho rangers. Perhaps working with horses and being much in the saddle has something to do with it as well. The packers, even in Idaho, are more like the cowpunchers; I always like to sit and visit with a bunch of packers.

One of the activities which has given me great pleasure and satisfaction as a forester is tree planting. As forest supervisor of the Lolo Forest I early established the Savenac Nursery, which was at one time the largest of the Forest Service nurseries, and which has for more than thirty-five years produced from two million to seven million young trees a year.[1]

Growing Trees

The great 1910 fires left millions of acres blackened and devastated, and it has been our job for years to restore such areas to productivity by artificial planting. Perhaps one reason why tree planting is a pleasant job is because spring planting is one of the earliest field activities of the year. As soon as the snow goes off the burns, in late April or early May, the planting crews are put out. When the weather is good, as it often is, May is one of the pleasantest months of the year to be in the hills. The sunshine is warm, there are no flies or mosquitoes, the spring flowers are in bloom, and all the trees and shrubs are dressed in new fresh green, and it seems good to be outdoors after a long winter. On a big planting operation, tent camps are established, usually for about fifty men. The mules are brought in from winter pasture, and the pack trains commence to move in supplies and equipment and bales and bales of burlap-packed bundles of young trees from the nursery. The planters work in crews of fifteen men, moving in echelon across a burned area, their mattocks rising and falling as they skillfully set the little trees, only six to eight inches high, in the moist and receptive ground.

The first three years after a plantation has been completed is always a discouraging period. The little trees are concealed or half smothered by brush and ferns and fire weed, and one wonders if many of them are surviving. Then perhaps four or five years after the planting job one comes back to find the trees have taken hold and are shooting up a foot or a foot and a half a year, and the whole hillside is covered with fine young pine seedlings. If one is fortunate one may come back again in thirty years and walk under the crowns of a splendid pole stand of vigorous young trees. Some of my oldest plantations are nearly thirty-five years old, and it is always a joy to see them and watch their development year by year. When a forester goes to St. Peter for a final accounting, I am sure that when he is asked what he has done with his life, if he can point to thousands of acres of once-ugly burn now covered with a growing forest, it will offset many sins of omission and commission.

I recall an amusing incident connected with a personally conducted trip with Idaho congressmen, D. Worth Clark[2] and Compton I. White Jr.[3] through some of the Idaho forests. Clark was a good and appreciative

FIG. 25. Elers Koch and visiting dignitaries at the Savenac Nursery in 1937. *Left to right:* Herbert A. Smith, senior Forest Service Information Officer; Koch; former chief Henry S. Graves; Fred E. Brown, district ranger on the Cabinet National Forest; and Gifford Pinchot, former chief and two-term Governor of Pennsylvania.

listener, and really wanted to know what was going on, but Comp White, who was none too friendly to the Forest Service, and was continually needling it, wanted to do all the talking himself. If a forest officer tried to tell him about some line of work, Comp immediately interrupted and started to lay down the law to him. We ended up one evening at the Priest River Experiment Station,[4] quite a party of us, and someone had been farsighted enough to bring along a couple of bottles of Scotch to refresh the party before dinner, after a big day in the field. When whoever was pouring the whiskey came to Comp, he waved his hand and said, "Pour me a good big one." So he got a water glass about two-thirds full and a little soda squirted on top. When we went in the cookhouse, everybody was feeling pretty good, and much lively talk was going on. I happened to be seated next to Mr. White at the table. I am a bit hard of hearing, and my right ear, which was next to Mr. White, is completely deaf. Comp was in fine fettle, and talked to me all through dinner about what the Forest Service ought to do. With the clatter of voices going on I could catch only an occasional word, but nodded and said, "Yes, yes," occasionally to show my interest. When he got up from the table, Comp remarked, "Well, I must say, you Forest Service men are good listeners."

I have been out with Senator Burton K. Wheeler[5] two or three times. He was generally friendly to the Forest Service, and ready to listen intelligently to what we might tell him. I had one curious experience with him, indicating the attitude congressmen sometimes have toward the expenditure of government funds. We had been having a very serious infestation of bark beetles in central Montana, which threatened to wipe out most of the lodgepole pine of that region. Under the advice of the Bureau of Entomology we had for years been trying to combat the infestation by spotting, cutting down, and burning the infested trees with the larval brood in them. This is often a successful measure if applied early enough, before the infestation becomes too widespread. We had been working at the control job for several years in the Bitterroot and Big Hole Valleys, and had expended over $200,000, when with the advice of entomologists we finally came to the conclusion, after a thorough survey, that the infestation had spread beyond our control, and only the course of nature would stop it. The last spring we had been working in the Big Hole Basin and had put out many control camps all through the adjacent timber. Naturally much of the money was for supplies, and a good deal of the wages of the men had gone to the stores, saloons, and hotels of the small towns of Wisdom and Jackson, and the local people were all for it. That summer Senator Wheeler, making the rounds of his constituency, had been through the Big Hole and talked to the local merchants. He got in touch with the forest supervisor, and I was called over to Butte to talk the matter over with the senator, who expressed great interest in the project. I was forced to tell him that we proposed to abandon the attempt, that we were convinced that we were pouring money in a rat hole, and we were not justified in asking for additional appropriations to continue the work. The senator waved that aside impatiently.

"I will be glad to help with this project, and I am sure I can get the necessary appropriations through the congressional committees," he said.

I repeated my argument.

"But, Senator," I said, "I think you don't understand. On the basis of our best judgment and our technical advice, it is not desirable to continue the work, and we don't want the money."

Senator Wheeler looked at me in amazement.

"Well," he said, "you are the first government man I ever talked to that didn't want an appropriation when he could get it."

Since the Forest Service is a bureau of the Department of Agriculture, we had some contact and an occasional visit from the various secretaries of agriculture. I remember a visit from old Tama Jim Wilson.[6] When he was out here in Montana he traveled with little publicity and the greatest simplicity, accompanied only by his son, who served as his secretary. It was quite a contrast to a visitation we had the previous month from James R. Garfield, the secretary of interior.[7] Garfield traveled in a special train, with much fanfare and a large entourage, and a following of newspaper men. I was privileged to ride through on the train from Missoula to Spokane and meet the great man.

Secretary of Agriculture Henry Wallace[8] was one of the most satisfactory big-time visitors we had. While one may not agree with his present political views, he is an extremely friendly and kindly man, interested in people, and an intelligent observer of the things the Forest Service tried to show him. We stopped over for luncheon at the Savenac Nursery, and after eating, Wallace spied a soft ball and bat one of the children around the place had left on the porch. He immediately proposed a baseball game, into which he entered with the greatest of spirit. I am a poor hand at ball, but Wallace knocked a high fly which fell into my hands, and I had the honor of catching out the secretary of agriculture.

Assistant Secretary Guy Tugwell was an interesting contrast to his chief.[9] I accompanied his party for two or three days on an inspection trip over some of the Idaho forests. Considering his reputation as a liberal, a defender of the people and champion of the underdog, I expected to see a man receptive to ideas, and interested in all the personal contacts he could make. To my surprise and disappointment, he was exceedingly stiff, unreceptive, and cold. I tried several times to explain certain things we saw on the trip of Forest Service activities but could hardly draw a spark of interest from him. When a forest supervisor or ranger was introduced to him, one would have expected he would try to draw him out and find out what sort of fellows these foresters were, but beyond a stiff handshake and "How do you do?" he rarely seemed to want to follow up the acquaintance. It looked to me that his interest in the welfare of people was purely academic, and for the individual he did not care a damn.

An amusing incident happened here a few years ago when Jim Farley[10] stopped off in Missoula to dedicate the new wing of the Federal Building. This wing was built primarily to accommodate the Forest Service and was occupied almost exclusively by that organization. A good-sized crowd, including practically all the employees of the Forest Service, gathered around the west steps of the new wing to hear Farley speak. Glen Smith, who happened to be acting regional forester at that time, made a short introductory speech. It was apparent that Farley was not listening to Smith's talk, but was rapidly leafing through his typewritten speech, which he had probably not seen before. While all of us Forest Service people stood openmouthed and expectant waiting for some words of praise and goodwill for the Forest Service, Farley read off his speech, which never even mentioned the Forest Service, but was all about the achievements of the Post Office Department. If ever a speech fell flat it was that one!

CHAPTER 10

Ranger Stories

Whenever a group of foresters get together around a campfire or around the bunkhouse stove of an evening, one can look for a continuous series of stories or references dropped casually from fields of action all over the West. One man begins, "When I was up in the Crazy Mountains," and another caps the story with "Back in 1910 when I was in the St. Joe country," and so it goes from mountain to forest to range land. But once get such a group started on bear stories, it seems that every man has his own favorite bear story. For some reason bear stories are always humorous. Unless a man gets really chewed and bitten by a bear, any experience with one is funny. The bear is the clown of the woods, at times shy, but sometimes as bold and impudent as a cocker spaniel pup, and even more destructive. A temporarily unoccupied tent camp or even a cabin is a constant temptation to a bear, and what he can do to the grub box and the bed in such a camp is indescribable. Even when occupied, the night raids of a bear on a camp lead to some pretty humorous situations.

I remember one time I pulled in to the Powell Ranger Station—at that time a remote spot in the heart of the Clearwater. Shortly after I arrived we heard an excited voice outside, and in burst Ole Olsen, the lookout man from Rocky Point, about fifteen miles from the ranger station. Ole was a young Swede or Norwegian—I forget which—and as white-headed as any Scandinavian you ever saw. He was all out of breath, and covered with dust and mud, and his face was as white as his hair. When he finally recovered his breath and got calmed down a bit, he told us his story.

He had come down from his lookout to his tent camp, which was at a spring about two hundred yards from the lookout point, to get his dinner. He walked up to the tent and threw the flap open, and to his horror, found himself face-to-face with a big brown bear. He said, "I slap him in the face with the water bag, and up I go up a tree." The first tree he came to was a two-foot spruce without any lower limbs, and he got only ten feet up, looking down despairingly at the bear, which reared against the tree, and then settled down to wait. Ole hung on as long as he could, and then slithered down the tree. "I throw the crosscut saw at the bear, and up I go up another tree." This time he selected a tree with limbs and climbed up out of reach of the bear. He stayed up the tree for an hour or two, and finally the bear disappeared, and he ventured to come down. Being hot and disheveled after the encounter, he went down to the spring to get a drink of water, when out of the alder brush around the spring, right in his face, burst two more bears—black ones this time. That was too much, and without waiting to get his packsack, Ole started down the trail and never stopped till he got to the ranger station.

We rode up there the next day, and found the camp a complete wreck, the tent in ribbons (a bear never goes out the tent door, but always slashes an opening through the canvas). The bed was torn to pieces and the grub box was complete destruction—even the tin cans punctured. We finally had to give up that lookout hill till we could build a tight cabin.

My own best bear story was somewhat similar, only I was the comic figure that time. I was up on Ramshorn Creek in the Tobacco Root Mountains, with Supervisor Walt Derrick and Ranger Rust, looking over some lodgepole pine timber we intended to put up for sale to a local sawmill. It was early in May and patches of snow still lay in the timber.

I was walking about fifty feet ahead of the others when I saw through the open timber ahead of me a big brown bear. (All bear are big in bear stories, but this one really was big.) I called back to Derrick, "Look at the bear up there." The black or brown bear is usually timid and ready to run when he sights a man, and I fully expected this one to turn tail. But this fellow stood facing me, champing his jaws, and regarding me with his little pig's eyes, and then to my amazement he started straight for me at a lumbering gallop. I hesitated for a minute, afraid to run, and at the last moment went for a tree. The nearest tree was a smooth lodgepole, and I went up about twelve feet on the first impulse. The bear came up to the base of the tree and stopped with a "Whoof," all his hair standing up along his back and looking pretty ferocious. I hung on with one arm and waved the other at him and yelled, but it didn't seem to scare him any. Knowing that bears can climb trees, I fully expected he would start up after me, and made up my mind if he did I would let go all holds and drop on him and hope to escape in the confusion. I threw my hat at him, but that didn't seem to have any effect. The bear would back off a bit, and then charge up to the base of the tree, growling and ruffling his back fur, just like an ugly dog. He finally backed up about fifty feet, and I slid down the tree, but no sooner had I hit the ground than he was right on my heels again, and up I went up another tree. By this time I was beginning to get a bit scared by the persistence of the animal, and called out to Derrick and Rust that they had better be doing something about it. So they got clubs, and advanced slowly up the trail, waving the clubs and yelling. The bear retreated a bit, and I slipped down and joined the others.

"We'd better be getting out of here," said Derrick.

"I'll be damned if I do until I get my hat," I said. "I've got a new twelve-dollar Stetson up there, and I'm not getting out without it."

So we maneuvered cautiously up the trail, with the bear charging around the woods, first on one side and then on the other, till I made a dash and recovered my hat, and we retreated in good order, leaving the bear to hold the battlefield. I have seen lots of bear in the woods, but I never saw a black or a brown act like that before. A grizzly will often stand his ground, but a black or brown usually runs as fast as he can.

Ranger Frank Liebig of Kalispell is one of the best storytellers.[1] He is retired now, as he was one of the oldest rangers on the district, and started work back in 1902 on the old Lewis and Clark Forest, which is now in Glacier Park. Frank was one of the best mountain men and frontiersmen in the country and equal to any situation. I got him to write down a couple of stories, and here they are just as he wrote them.

"On one trip coming in across Gunsight Pass, I came in late one evening into Sperry Glacier Basin with my horses, ready to set up my tent for the night. I saw a crowd of people a little ways off and heard someone saying, 'There is the ranger now.' And soon people came running over and said a woman had fallen into a crevasse in Sperry Glacier[2] and they didn't know how to get her out. In the meantime they had sent a man down to the hotel ten miles away to get some rope. No telephone in the Forest yet. The first telephone was installed from Belton to the hotel in 1910.

"When the people told me about the woman falling into the crevasse, I turned the horses loose in a hurry, and grabbed two lash ropes and an axe, and told the men to come on. The place was a quarter of a mile to the edge of the glacier, and some 250 yards across the ice to the crevasse. I cut a stunted green fir four or five inches in diameter and five feet long, and had the men pack it along. When we got to the place three or four men stood at the place where the woman slid in. Two women and three or four men came along, with them a minister of the gospel by the name of Falls—a real mountaineer. He died in Seattle two years later. I selected a place on the lower side of the crevasse, and set the green post into the hole and packed ice all around it to make it fairly solid. Then I tied the two lash ropes together and tied a number of knots in the rope for a good handhold. Then I tied the rope to the post sticking above the ice and told a couple of men to hang onto the post so it wouldn't slip out, and threw the rope into the crevasse.

"I could see the woman lying almost horizontal in the ice. The crevasse was four or five feet wide at the top, and came together to a knife edge at the bottom, about thirty-five feet down. She was wedged in at about thirty feet and dead as a doornail (so I thought).

"I slid down the rope and had some sweat worked up, and when I got down, was it cold! I tried to hang onto the rope and pull the woman loose but couldn't budge her. The walls of the ice were smooth as glass and I could not get a foothold. I thought she was dead anyway, so I stepped on her body to rest my feet, and told the men to haul up the rope and send the axe down, which they did. Then I chopped a hole on each side of the ice big enough to put my feet in for a hold, and then sent the axe up again to the top. When the rope came down again I started to pull the woman loose and nearly pulled her arm out, she was wedged in so tight with her fall and then my standing on her body. But I finally got her loose, having a foothold chopped in the ice, then managed to get the rope around her waist and the men pulled her up to the surface, and then let the rope down again.

"I was so frozen by this time I was in doubt that I could climb the rope, so I put it under my arms and was hauled up by the men too. When I got out I could hardly stand up I was so cold, and had to stamp around a bit to get my blood in circulation again.

"We had plenty of help by this time. Someone brought a lantern and candles from the camp, and it was getting dark. There was no stretcher, so four men got hold of the woman, one on each leg and one on each arm, one ahead with a lantern. When we got to the edge of the ice there was a narrow trail leading down through the rocks and around some cliffs, one over twenty feet high. We thought it would be safer for all of us to let the body down on our rope over the cliff. Someone went ahead to receive the body below. When the body was halfway down the woman began to spin around and hit her head on the rocks, cutting quite a gash in her head, which must have brought her to. Because she let out an awful yell, which scared us half to death, as we all thought she was a goner sure. Then she fainted again.

"We got her to camp finally, where they had a big fire going and lots of hot coffee and lots more hot drinks, and we all had our share of hot brandy. Even the minister of the gospel and yours truly, even if I was on the water wagon. I had my share and don't know today how I got into my sleeping bag only half undressed. I think someone must have helped me.

"A doctor came up towards morning and pronounced the woman

O.K. Some men and women filled her up all night with hot brandy until she was gloriously drunk. We sure had a late breakfast next day. All thought I had done a wonderful job. But I pulled out ahead of the crowd in order not to attract so much attention. I didn't even stop at the hotel and went direct to the ranger station. The woman never even said thank you for getting her out of the glacier. She surely would have been dead if she had stayed in the ice all night. But such is the world."

Frank had a lot of bear and lion stories too, but his goat story was really unusual. Here it is:

"I always had a craze to have a pet bear or deer or something around the station. In 1905 or 1906, Supervisor F. N. Haines and myself made a trip after Christmas to Avalanche Lake³ to see if a bridge could be built across the creek without too much expense. At the head of Lake McDonald we had about a foot of snow, but near Avalanche Lake there was about three feet of snow and we had to use our snowshoes. When we got to the foot of the lake we saw a bunch of mountain goats crossing the ice, going from one shore to another. The goats had a regular trail though the deep snow, only their backs sticking above the snow once in a while.

"I said to the supervisor, 'Here is a chance to take home a live goat without too much trouble.' Mr. Haines was skeptical, and said I couldn't handle one of the big goats alone. If I picked a real small one we might get one to the station between us two. I told him, 'Just watch my smoke.' I was in good shape in them days and didn't take my hat off for nobody.

"Anyhow, I cut across with my snowshoes and headed the goats off before they reached the shore, and fell on the nearest goat that was handy, and it happened to be a good-sized one at that. There was no time for selection. In that narrow trench there were goats everywhere, one climbing over another to get away. I thought I surprised the goats, but the surprise was on me. I was on top of the goat when I started, trying to hang onto his head; the next thing I know I was on the bottom and the goat on top. I had snow and goat hair and whatnot in my eyes and down my neck. He tried his darndest to hook me with his sharp horns, and I had my hands full to keep him from hooking me in the face or other parts of my body. His feet got tangled in my snowshoes and tore

175

most of the webbing out. Half of my pants and coat was already gone when the supervisor came up to help me. But what did he do? Lay down in the snow and laughed till the tears ran down his cheeks, and me getting more mad every minute. Finally one snowshoe came off, and not long after the other. After that I could handle him better, and straddled his back and just watched out for his horns. He could kick like a mule, but his hoofs weren't as sharp as those of a deer. I rode the blooming goat back and forth in the ditch till he was plumb petered out, and the supervisor yelling 'Ride him, cowboy!'

"I told the supervisor to bring my packsack and what was left of my pants. I had some rope in the packsack, and fixed up one of the broken snowshoes and tied a piece of rope around his horns and one piece around his hind leg. I thought we could lead him home. It worked fine in the deep snow on the ice and while the goat was still petered out. But when we hit the timber and solid footing the goat changed tactics. Once or twice the supervisor couldn't hold onto his rope, and the goat charged me, and I had the choice either to play hide and seek behind a tree or lose another piece of my pants, which, by the way, the supervisor said, 'Belonged to the Adam and Eve variety.' I finally tried to put my coat over his head. I thought he would lead better; and in the shuffle the rope came off his hind leg, which the supervisor had to hang onto to keep him from running me over. After the rope came off he was too dangerous to handle, so after he got tangled up in the brush with the rope on his horns I managed to cut the rope and set him free. It was just as well. If we had had to tug the goat another mile we would have no clothes left on us except our rubbers and socks, and they were all wringing wet."

CHAPTER 11

The Forest Service and the New Deal

From its very inception, the Forest Service was always a thrifty and economical organization. There was so much to do that we knew needed to be done, and so little funds to do it with, that everyone carried in his mind constantly the necessity of making each dollar go as far as possible. There was a continual and scientific study of every operation, with the intent of cutting out all surplus personnel motion, and doing each job in the most effective and cheapest way. Such mechanical operations as forest nursery work were subjected to minute analysis, with stopwatch records of each process, step by step, and consideration of methods and equipment, until the work was reduced to a minimum of cost.

Rangers' and supervisors' diaries were analyzed to determine whether the work was being done in orderly sequence to involve the least possible loss by unnecessary travel or waste time. Every man's job was analyzed and broken down into its constituent parts so that a work plan as detailed as possible could be made.

The economy principle was continuously held before the personnel. It applied to buildings and structures and roads and trails and telephone lines, as well as the use of time. A supervisor was as apt to be reprimanded for building a trail better than necessary for the use it was to be put as he would be for building it not good enough. On the whole the Forest Service had a well-earned reputation among government bureaus and with the public for economy and efficiency and making every dollar of appropriations count.

Then came the Depression of the thirties, and with the new administration a flood of public works and drive for employment of idle men. The Forest Service was in an excellent position to participate in this movement at once. We had ready extensive plans for needed improvement of the public property in the national forests, which had only been waiting adequate appropriations. We needed more and better ranger stations, lookout towers, telephone lines, roads, trails, and bridges, and there was an immense reservoir of urgently needed work in blister rust control to protect the valuable white pine in Idaho and Montana from imminent destruction by a rapidly spreading disease.

As a result of our readiness to accept it, the Forest Service was flooded with more men and money than we had hoped to get by regular appropriations for many years. The first large-scale spending was what was known as Emergency Relief Administration (ERA) funds.[1] That was good money. There were practically no restrictions on the use of it beyond ordinary appropriations except that the forty-hour week was introduced, and for some unaccountable reason, the going scale of wages was increased. But the money could be used without restriction for the purchase of equipment, materials, and overhead necessary for well-balanced projects, and a great deal was accomplished in the way of improving Forest Service property. It was the best-expended money that went into the New Deal employment drive.

Then came the CCC, the Civilian Conservation Corps.[2] Much has been written about the CCC, most of it favorable. The project appealed to people, and in its conception was a fine thing. One of the most distressing phases of a period of general unemployment is the situation of youths who are just ready to start working, and finding no jobs available for them, fall into unprofitable idleness. The CCC solved that problem for many thousands of young men and was from that point of view wholly good. There were, however, many phases of the administration and regulations set up for its control that are subject to criticism, and that materially reduced the value and efficiency of the CCC. The army was made responsible for the general administration of the CCC camps, the assembly and transportation of the boys, moving them into camps, and the feeding, care, discipline, and payment of the boys. These camps, usually two hundred boys to the camp, were turned over to the work agencies, the Forest Service, national parks, Soil Conservation Service, state forestry departments, etc., the work agency being wholly responsible for planning and supervising the boys the army turned over to them, after holding out what they considered necessary for camp operation.

The army has received much unmerited praise for its work in handling the CCC. It is perhaps ungracious for a man who was one of the cooperating agencies working with the army to be critical, but while the army end of the job eventually settled down into a fairly competent management, the first movement of the men into the camps and the administration of the first six months was so confused and lacking in carefully worked out plans that I often wondered how the army could possibly mobilize millions of men for war if they could not handle a few thousand CCCs in a more competent and plan-wise manner.

The movement to the camps started in the spring of 1933. The Forest Service in Montana and Idaho had fifty or sixty camps. We were responsible for the location of the camps, subject to the approval of the army, for having the work projects planned, providing a superintendent for each camp, and the necessary foremen, and furnishing the necessary tools, equipment, and materials for the project work. The army had the immediate job, when the boys arrived on the ground, of setting up tent camps for sleeping and living quarters, and building a large mess hall for feeding two hundred men, and a bathhouse. Since this was a uniform requirement for thousands of camps going in all over the United States, one would naturally have expected that the army would arrive with a complete set of plans and blueprints for each building, bills of materials, and a well-selected supply of carpenter and other tools for the construction work. To our amazement, they had nothing of the sort, and each army officer in charge was frantically drawing plans and trying to make up orders for lumber, pipe, etc., with little general knowledge of the grades, specifications, and requirements. In most cases they arrived with no adequate tools to work with. I recall one camp that came in with two tool chests, which when opened contained two pipe wrenches—nothing more. In some of the camps the summer was practically over before they had the tents properly set and the two simple buildings completed, which of course meant that a large percentage of the crew had to be retained for camp work rather than released for project work. If the Forest Service had not stepped in beyond its requirements and furnished tools and help from our superintendents and foremen, I doubt if some of the camps would have been completed.

The arrangements for feeding the boys were very poor. Especially for the first six months the food was terrible, badly cooked and usually served half cold. There were no expert cooks supplied, not even to train some of the CCC boys to do the cooking, and one can imagine what those boys did to good food. Even after the camps were settled down and had been operating for a couple of years, the food was rarely good. I have eaten many CCC meals, but I can say I never enjoyed one in the way I enjoy a meal in the field at a logging camp or a Forest Service mess.

When the camps arrived they had the most inadequate cooking and mess equipment, only small portable ranges, and no dishes except the mess kits issued to each boy. The Forest Service got busy and helped to beg, borrow, or steal adequate cooking ranges from our friends in the lumber industry, which was largely shut down by the Depression, but it was months before the boys could sit down properly to a table with regular dishes. Naturally the poor food did not help morale, and our foremen, accustomed to good logging camp food, were almost to desperation. If work had not been so scarce that year I doubt if we could have held most of them. The boys were, in general, well clothed by the army, but we had a battle that lasted for months about adequate footgear for working in the woods. The boys had regular army leather-soled shoes, all right around the barracks, but any woodsman who has attempted to work on steep slopes or about logs in slick-soled leather shoes knows he is practically a cripple. We begged and implored that the army furnish calks, or at least hobnails, for the shoes of the boys, but it took months, and sometimes years, before they were so equipped. It seems to me unbelievable that the army should know or care so little about proper equipment for outdoor work. It may seem a small thing, but I believe the lack of proper woods boots cut down efficiency of the crews by twenty or twenty-five percent the first summer.

Only a few of the camps in this district were filled with local boys; the majority of them were shipped in from the East. I inspected many of the camps the first summer and found an almost infallible gauge for determining at first sight whether or not it was a good crew. If there was a high percentage of blondes among the boys I expected good results; if they were mostly brunettes, not so good. That does not mean that the blondes were necessarily better workers than brunettes; there were two steps further in the deduction. The crews with mostly black-haired boys were usually largely Jewish or Italian boys from New York and New Jersey, and the significance of it was not that they were Italian or Jewish, but that they had never learned to work outdoors, whereas the camps with a considerable mixture of blondes often came from country or smalltown districts. We had two all Negro camps, not southern Negroes, but boys from Harlem. They were the most unskilled of all and accomplished little work. It was amusing to be in the vicinity of these camps. They were located way back on the Coeur d'Alene Forest at the end of a road, and while they were in there, to see nothing but black boys walking the trails or bathing in the streams gave the impression of being suddenly let down in Africa.[3]

After the first summer more permanent camps were built with barracks for the boys, recreation halls, etc. The regular army officers were mostly released (most of them heartily disliked the assignment) and replaced by reserve officers who really wanted the job, and we got down to very good working relations with the army.

One thing that made it difficult to get the most efficient work from the CCC camps was the necessity of always working the boys from the large central camps. We did finally get permission to put in some side camps of forty or fifty boys, but they had to be built from Forest Service funds, and had to be almost as elaborate as the main camps. It was almost impossible to use them on short-term jobs like a tree planting operation, where we were accustomed to establish a temporary tent camp for perhaps three weeks, with only essential facilities for sleeping and eating. The army would not permit the CCC boys to be employed in such primitive camps, though they were the customary facility for the men we hired as tree planters. We also urgently needed men for trail maintenance, but that requires small, rapidly moving crews of five to ten men, and we could not detach the boys for such service, though it would have been far better for the boys than barracks life. The result of all these restrictions was that in many cases relatively low-priority work, which could be handled from the large camps, had to be given preference over much higher-priority work, which required more mobile crews. On the whole the boys were babied too much for their own good or the good of the work. It cost approximately $1,200 a year to maintain a CCC boy in the camps, and in my best judgment the work accomplished per boy was equivalent to about $300 to $400 in regular appropriations. We used to figure on blister rust control work that two of our regular thirty-man crews would do more and better work than a full two-hundred-man CCC camp.

It was the responsibility of the Forest Service to provide for each CCC camp a superintendent and the necessary number of foremen, usually seven to ten. With the rush of camps moving in the spring of 1933 we had to do some scurrying around to employ and train so many men for overhead. Fortunately for us the logging industry was at low ebb, and the lumber companies were delighted to have us take off their hands a large number of their camp foremen and logging superintendents, who made excellent men for the job. No sooner had we got our camps manned with overhead and running with a reasonable degree of efficiency, when the politicians suddenly discovered that here were hundreds of jobs being given out with no sign of patronage. It was too big a plum to resist. Up to that time there had been no vestige of political influence in selection of personnel in the Forest Service. All of the permanent positions were under the civil service, and in all my period of service I had never seen a man hired, appointed, or promoted for any other reason than that he appeared to be the best available man for the job. This throwing of Forest Service employment into the political field was extremely distasteful to us. The Democratic congressmen insisted that with the Democratic administration in power, it was outrageous that so many Republicans were being appointed, and in this region insisted on an investigation. The funny part of it was that when a check was made of the foremen and their politics, it turned out that we did have many more Republicans than Democrats, a reasonable explanation being that most of these men were recruited from the lumber industry, which is usually inclined to be on the Republican side. I had a good deal to do with the selection of superintendents and foremen, and positively know that the question of a man's politics never entered the situation at all, nor did we have the slightest interest or knowledge of whether the men selected were Democrats or Republicans, but we never could convince some of the Democratic congressmen that we had not deliberately stuffed the CCC with Republicans.

At any rate our free selection was over, and all camp overhead had to be selected from what were euphemistically known as "advisor's lists," men endorsed by the local representatives or senators of the Democratic Party. It was a severe blow to the morale of the Forest Service, which had so long been free from political appointments.

The Works Progress Administration (WPA) followed closely on the heels of the CCC.[4] It may have been a method by which the largest possible number of men were given employment of a sort with the least expenditure of funds, but from the standpoint of getting any accomplishments of value for the public money expended, a worse system could hardly have been devised. The Forest Service received allotments of considerable amounts of WPA money, and we did our best to do something of value with it, but the allotments were made in such a way that anything but the barest sort of hand labor was impossible, and in these days there is very little work that can be done economically solely with hand labor. Under the terms of the allotment, for each dollar paid out for wages for the men, only a very small percentage was allotted for overhead, skilled labor, tools and equipment, transportation, or materials. Anything in the nature of road construction, which required machinery, or any building, which required materials, was impossible. Gradually the WPA crews fell into mostly low-priority hand labor jobs, such as cleaning up roadsides, work which had some value but was distinctly low in priority, with many other much more urgent projects needing to be undertaken.

I recall once passing a WPA crew of two hundred men employed by one of the counties in Idaho at widening a highway road cut with shovels and wheelbarrows. I remarked to my companion, "Look at that now. Here they are employing two hundred men, and if they were using road machinery only about twenty would have jobs."

My friend remarked sarcastically, "Yes, and if they used teaspoons instead of shovels they might use two thousand men."

Naturally both the men and the overhead fell into a more-or-less hopeless attitude. If employment was all that was wanted and accomplishment did not count for much, why push the job, and as everybody knows, the work fell into a very leisurely pace.

While I do not pretend to be an economist, it has always seemed to me that if the WPA money had been put into ordinary public works, roads, buildings, dams, etc., which were badly needed, the results would have been far better. It is true that not so many men would have been placed directly on the payroll, but orders for cement and lumber and steel and tools and machinery are very quickly translated back into labor elsewhere, and in the long run such a plan would have given the depressed industry of the country more of an impulse than the hopeless dole of WPA wages.

The Forest Service received much material benefit from the New Deal outpouring of funds through the CCC and WPA. By sheer weight of manpower many greatly needed improvements were made in the public property of the national forests. However most of us knew that half the money so expended by normal appropriations would have produced even greater results. It certainly had a very profound and undesirable effect on the morale and principles of the Forest Service, and doubtless other government bureaus who participated in the relief work, from which they have not yet fully recovered. After these years of plenty, the organization has never come back to its stern principles of economy and frugality. One of the old-time rangers once remarked to me that the CCC and the WPA had permanently ruined half the good foremen in the country, and it was not only the foremen but government officials all the way up the line that were subtly influenced. It is probable that the expanded government bureaus will never get back to the simplicity and economy that characterized them before the New Deal.

It is perhaps natural that we old-timers are inclined to criticize. The general expansion of government activities and government spending is somewhat difficult for us to keep pace with, when we look back on the relative simplicity of the earlier days. After five years' retirement I still keep in close touch with the Forest Service, and I firmly believe it is still one of the most efficient and public-service minded bureaus in the entire government organization. In spite of all the modern foofaraw which may have been attached, it is still the same old Forest Service I grew up with.

Which reminds me of a favorite story in this region that illustrates my point. It is about old Jim Ward, one of our pioneer rangers, who came out west from the Minnesota woods before there were any modern trains. When he finally decided to go back to Minnesota to visit his old tillicums, he made up his mind he was going in style, and bought a first-class ticket in a Pullman car. He rode all day, and was due to arrive at his station in Minnesota early the next morning. I will try to tell the story in his own words.

"When it came time to go to bed," he said, "they was double-deck bunks, and I had a lower bunk. I pulled off my old shoes and put them under the bunk and rolled in. There was green curtains in front of the bunk and a little hammock in front of the window, but I didn't know what that was for. It was a good soft bed and I went right to sleep, and the first thing I know the porter was shaking me and says we are at my station, and I'd have to get off quick. So I pulled on my pants and reached under the bunk for my shoes, and they was gone. They was a pair of nice shiny black shoes there that belonged to some other fellow, but I couldn't find my old shoes nowhere. Just then the conductor hollered 'All aboard!' and I knowed I had no more time, so I says to myself, 'Old fellow, you are going to be out of luck,' and I slips on them new shoes and grabbed my packsack, and got off the train just in time. I run down the street half a block, and thinks I'll stop and tie my shoelaces. I looked at them shoes, and I looked at them again, and do you know, they was my own god damned shoes!"

CHAPTER 12

The Passing of the Lolo Trail

The Lolo Trail is no more.

The bulldozer blade has ripped out the hoof tracks of Chief Joseph's ponies. The trail was worn deep by centuries of Nez Perce and Blackfeet Indians, by Lewis and Clark, by companies of Northwest fur traders, by General Howard's cavalry horses, by Captain Mullan, the engineer, and by the early-day forest ranger. It is gone, and in its place there is only the print of the automobile tire in the dust.

What of the camps of fragrant memory—Camp Martin, Rocky Ridge, Noseeum Meadows, Bald Mountain, Indian Grave, Howard Camp, Indian Post Office, Spring Mountain, Cayuse Junction, Packer Meadows? No more will the traveler unsaddle his ponies to roll and graze on the bunch grass of the mountaintops. No more "the mule train coughing in the dust." The trucks roll by on the new Forest Service road, and the old camps are no more than a place to store spare barrels of gasoline.

No more will the mountain man ride the high ridges between the Kooskooskee and the Chopunnish, "smoking his pipe in the mountains, sniffing the morning cool."

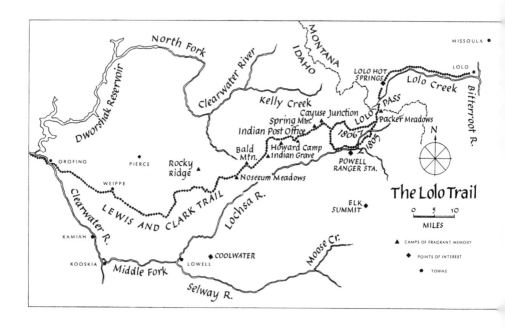

FIG. 26. Map of the Lolo Trail, from Lolo Pass to Weippe, which Lewis and Clark traversed in 1805 and 1806; here it is related to the region's rivers, Koch's "camps of fragrant memory," and selected towns.

The Passing of the Lolo Trail

It is now but three hours' drive from the streets of Missoula to the peak where Captain Lewis smoked his pipe and wrote in his journal: "From this elevated spot we have a commanding view of the surrounding mountains, which so completely enclose us that though we have once passed them, we almost despair of ever escaping from them without the assistance of the Indians." Only ten years ago it was just as Lewis and Clark saw it.

So it is everywhere.

The hammer rings in the CCC camp on the remotest waters of the Selway. The bulldozer snorts on Running Creek, that once limit of the back of beyond. The moose at Elk Summit lift their heads from the lilypads to gaze at the passing motor truck. Major Penn's beloved Coolwater Divide has become a motor road.

No more can one slip up to the big lick at Powell on a frosty October morning and see the elk in droves. The hunters swarm in motorcars in the public campgrounds.

And all to what end? Only a few years ago the great Clearwater wilderness stretched from the Bitterroot to Kooskia, from the Cedar Creek mines to the Salmon River and beyond. No road and no permanent human habitation marred its primitive nature. There it lay—the last frontier—an appeal to the mind of a few adventurous souls who might wish to penetrate its fastness and plunge for weeks beyond human communication.

The Forest Service sounded the note of progress. It opened up the wilderness with roads and telephone lines and airplane landing fields. It capped the mountain peaks with white-painted lookout houses, laced the ridges and streams with a network of trails and telephone lines, and poured in thousands of fire fighters year after year in a vain attempt to control forest fires.

Has all this effort and expenditure of millions of dollars added anything to human good? Is it possible that it was all a ghastly mistake, like plowing up the good buffalo grass sod of the dry prairies? Has the country as it stands now as much human value as it had in the nineties when Major Penn's forest rangers first rode into it?

To answer the questions let us first examine what manner of country this is and what it is good for. I have before me a map of north Idaho made up on the basis of the combined judgment of the best qualified forest officers, which shows in green Zone 1, the area of unquestioned value for timber production; in white Zone 2, areas which may possibly have some future timber productive value; and in yellow Zone 3 areas which owing to altitude, rugged topography, permanent inaccessibility, or inferior timber growth, will never, so far as best present judgment indicates, come into the picture as timber producing land.

The three northern national forests in the state are considerably cut up as to zones, but with green and white greatly predominating on the map. Farther south the picture changes. The upper reaches of the North Fork of the Clearwater, the Lochsa, Selway, and Salmon Rivers form a great solid block of yellow Zone 3 on the map, covering 3,000 square miles, or two million acres in round numbers. This is a different geological formation. Departing from the Precambrian shales of the north end of the state, this is part of the great granite batholith of central Idaho. It is a country of deep canyons, rushing, boulder-strewn rivers, mountain lakes, and high peaks. The decomposed granite soil is thin, coarse-grained, and shallow. Prior to the intervention of the Forest Service, the tide of civilization surged round it, and few men entered it. Elk, moose, mountain goats, deer, and fur bearers maintained a natural existence, protected by the country itself.

It seems obvious that whatever value the area may have, it is not for timber production. Rather its value lies in whatever pleasure man may get out of its recreational resources in the way of isolation, scenery, fish, and game.

I would that I could turn the clock back and make a plea for preserving the area as it was twenty-five or even five years ago. Alas, it is too late. Roads are such final and irretrievable facts.

The Forest Service built these hundreds of miles of road and these thousands of miles of trail and telephone line for one purpose only—to facilitate the suppression of forest fires.

The whole history of the Forest Service's attempt to control fire in the backcountry of the Selway and Clearwater is one of the saddest chapters in the history of a high-minded and efficient public service. In the face of the most heroic effort and the expenditure of millions of dollars and several lives, this country has been swept again and again by most-uncontrollable conflagrations. The Lochsa Canyon is burned and reburned from Pete King to Jerry Johnson, and the Selway from the Forks to Moose Creek.

Many fires have been controlled, but when the time is ripe for a conflagration, man's efforts have been puny in the face of nature's forces. I am not criticizing the efforts of others. I have personally taken part in four major fire campaigns on the Lochsa River, in 1910, 1919, 1929, and 1934. Each year we made a greater effort and threw larger forces of men into the battle, but so far as results were concerned there is little difference between 1919, when crews of thirty or forty men, in a vain but courageous gesture, were trailing the leeward end of each of five or six gigantic fires, and 1934, when fire fighters were counted in thousands, and the fires swept 180,000 acres.

When fire gets a good start in the dry fire-killed cedar and white fir of the Selway and burning conditions are just right, the whole United States Army, if it was on the ground, could do nothing but keep out of the way. After years of experience I have come to the considered conclusion that control of fire in the backcountry of the Selway and Lochsa drainages is a practical impossibility. I firmly believe that if the Forest Service had never expended a dollar in this country since 1900 there would have been no appreciable difference in the area burned over. It is even possible that, by extinguishing fires in favorable seasons which would have run over a few hundred or a few thousand acres, the stage was only set for the greater conflagrations which went completely beyond fire-line control. After all, this country existed and maintained a general timber cover before man was born and for millions of years before the Forest Service came into being. Surely its existence as wild land capable of sheltering its game and holding the watershed together cannot now be altogether dependent on the efforts of the Forest Service. No important new element has been introduced. Not a single one of the greater fires which have swept the country since 1910 has been man-caused. And even 130 years ago we have Lewis and Clark's testimony that the Indians habitually set fire for such a trivial purpose as to insure fair weather for a journey.

Since the two-million-acre unit under consideration is now part of five national forests—the Selway, Nez Perce, Clearwater, Lolo, and Bitterroot—it is difficult to segregate past costs of administration in this country.

The records show that since 1912 the Selway Forest alone has expended the vast sum of $3,065,000 for all purposes, with receipts of only $76,000. This does not include the present year's cost, which must have amounted to over half a million dollars. The Selway expenditures for the past four fiscal years, 1931 to 1934, have averaged $288,000 annually. If the expenditures by the four other national forests within the low-value zone are added to the Selway, it is probable that the Forest Service has sunk at least five million dollars to date in the area, and will continue to expend at the rate of $200,000 to $300,000 a year, with practically no hope of timber sale receipts or more than a trivial amount in grazing fees to offset the expenditures. What is the future line of action which should be taken by the Forest Service in this country? There seem to be three alternatives:

1. Continue on about the present basis with some gradual extension of roads, trails, landing fields, and other facilities and about the present force of protection men.

2. If Congress can be induced to appropriate necessary funds, greatly intensify the protection setup, open all the remaining inaccessible country with roads, and greatly increase the protection forces.

3. Set up a carefully defined unit of about two million acres as a low-value area which does not justify the cost of fire control. Maintain only existing roads and the major trails. Withdraw the entire fire-control organization and retain only a police force of two or three rangers to protect the game and direct recreational use.

The first alternative has been found by twenty years' experience to be practically useless. It has resulted in greatly modifying and to a large extent destroying the special values of a unique and distinctive wilderness area. The results in fire control have been almost negligible. Every really bad fire season has seen great conflagrations sweep completely beyond control, nullifying the results of every fire extinguished in the more favorable seasons. If I could show in color a map of this region with the areas burned over since the beginning of national forest administration, the country would be shocked at the lack of results for the millions expended.

The second alternative, a greatly increased intensification of protection, appears at least more logical than the first. We are now making vast expenditures with little or no results. To double or treble these expenditures and get the desired results would at least give the taxpayers something for their money. It would mean abandoning the wilderness area completely and opening the whole country with roads, but that has already progressed so far that there is really no wilderness left, and perhaps we might as well make up our minds to an automobile recreational use of this area rather than a primitive packhorse use, provided we are going to tackle the protection job.

The question then arises, even with the most intensive protection system conceivable, can the recurrence of such conflagrations as in 1934, 1929, 1919, and 1910 be prevented? The Selway country presents the toughest fire-control conditions of any area in the United States. There is a combination of very dry, hot summer with the worst fuel conditions imaginable. The forest in the lower country and along streams is largely a cedar, white-fir mixture, much of it already fire-killed, and when a fire gets under way in such a stand on a bad fire day, look out! Dry cedar, much of it hollow in the center, is an extremely light and inflammable fuel. The hollow trees carry fire like a chimney; the trees fall and shatter into kindling, and the kindling springs to flames. At the same time shreds of dry cedar bark and sparks from rotten white fir snags throw fire to unbelievable distances ahead.

Can any conceivable system get the best of such conditions? In 1934 the four or five lightning fires which started in the lower Lochsa River drainage presented as favorable a setup for fire-control facilities as the most fantastic conception of an organization could provide. The fire which did most of the damage started right under the eye of several lookouts. Thousands of men in blister-rust crews, road crews, and CCC camps were working within a few hours' travel. An excellent road system traversed the area, making it possible to locate most of the fire camps on roads. In spite of the use of all these facilities and the rushing in of the best and most experienced fire overhead in the region, four fires got completely beyond control and swept an area of 180,000 acres. If similar circumstances arose next year or ten years from now it is not at all likely that any different results could be secured in this particular country. I can only conclude that by doubling or trebling the fire-control cost, the Forest Service might possibly reduce the area burned, but with always the possibility of a great conflagration sweeping beyond all control and nullifying all past efforts.

Even assuming the practicability of a fair degree of fire control through greatly increased expenditures, is the game worth the candle? The Forest Service men are a tough outfit and it takes a lot to make them admit they are licked, but the amount of taxpayers' money involved is so great that no false pride or saving of face should prevent a scrutiny of the justification of maintaining such expenditures when weighed against the values obtained, even though it involves an admission of defeat.

Almost any forester or lumberman would agree that the character of tree growth, soil, and topography on the area in question is such that there is little likelihood of its being developed commercially in the future, even under a period of considerable timber scarcity; and even though a few of the best areas should some time in the future be logged, the return would at best be far below the annual expenditures, to say nothing of interest on past investment.

Recreational use and watershed protection are the only other values to be considered. It is conceded that these values would be enhanced by control of fires. However, the country in question in its natural state before the intervention of the Forest Service supported a fair forest cover and did not show any serious indications of watershed injury. Its special recreational values were probably greater than they are after thirty years of Forest Service management.

This leads up then to the third alternative of withdrawing all fire control forces, stopping further expenditure for that purpose, and leaving the country pretty much to the forces of nature. It is a radical proposal, and could far better have been adopted ten years ago before the period of road construction started. Be that as it may, if a mistake has been made it is better to recognize it and change the mistaken policy than to plunge blindly ahead because a certain line of action has been started.

Much has been said and written about the abandonment of submarginal agricultural land. Should it not also be recognized that there is such a thing as submarginal forest land? Proper land classification and planning should lead us to radically different treatment of the wide range in classes of forest land. The good land will merit intensive treatment, the less-good land less cultivation, and the least-good lands something entirely different.

There has been enough money sunk, with little return, in the low-grade Selway wilderness to have acquired all the good cut-over and second-growth private forest land in Idaho, which is now a motherless orphan; and under the present plans the Selway wilderness will annually swallow up enough funds for intensive management of these good forest lands.

Suppose the Forest Service should go to the proper committee in Congress and say, "We can save $300,000 a year by withdrawing from attempted protection of two million acres of low-grade land in Idaho. Permit us to use this amount for the acquisition, management, protection, and planting of two million acres of the best Idaho land." Wouldn't that sound like a reasonable thing to do?

The objection may be made that public opinion would not permit withdrawal of fire control from this area. Some day public opinion may rend the Forest Service for having accomplished so little protection for so much money. Public opinion can be molded, and it is the job of foresters to lead public opinion in the right direction in forestry matters. Both as citizens and public officials it is the duty of responsible men in the Forest Service to use the public funds wisely, and not to advocate expenditures that do not yield reasonable returns.

I am not advocating withdrawing protection from all low-value forest lands. It is conceded that it is a misfortune whenever fire sweeps any forested area, and while it is difficult to measure that damage in dollars it is certainly worth an expenditure within limits to prevent such fires. If the Forest Service could be assured of a reasonably adequate control of fire in the Selway country for two or three hundred thousand dollars a year I am inclined to believe it would be worthwhile, even with little or no money return in sight. The trouble is that this country presents such an unusually difficult fire-control problem that even twice or thrice that amount will not insure any considerable reduction in the area which would burn without the attempted control, and a commonsense weighing of all factors indicates that it is time to withdraw from a losing game before more millions are expended with little or no results.

ACKNOWLEDGMENTS

As with any book project, this annotated edition of *Forty Years a Forester* would never have seen the light of day without a host of people very committed to its publication. First and foremost is Peter R. Koch, who wanted a new generation of readers to discover his grandfather's iconic memoir. A fine art printer and, like other members of his family before him, a distinguished collector of western Americana, Peter has an exquisite archive of rare manuscripts, documents, and images. He and his colleagues Jonathan Gerken and Dina Pollack made these available to me at a moment's notice. All the photographs and maps that illustrate this volume come from Peter's repository. I would never have known about this treasure trove, or of Peter's ambitions for *Forty Years a Forester*, had not he and I been in separate contact with Cheryl Hughes of the National Museum of Forest Service History in Missoula, Montana. She made the introduction and has remained an indefatigable cheerleader for the book. So has John Maclean, who graciously penned the foreword, and who, like his father Norman Maclean, has a keen understanding of Koch's formative role in the history of the Forest Service in the northern Rockies. I am once more indebted to the Forest History Society and its remarkable staff—Jason Howard, Eben Lehman, and Jamie Lewis—for their quick responses to all my questions. The University of Nebraska Press, particularly senior acquisitions editor Bridget Barry, has made the editorial process seamless. Recognizing the contribution that *Forty Years a Forester* might make to Bison Books, the press's award-winning imprint, she shepherded the manuscript through in-house and external review. I am as beholden to her and her colleagues in editorial and marketing as to the anonymous readers whose constructive criticism has made this a much stronger text. Closer to home, I have been the privileged recipient of a year-long sabbatical from Pomona College in 2017–18 so that I might work on this and other initiatives. Even more fortunate is that Judi Lipsett, my wife, best friend, and fellow traveler, once again has helped me resolve a number of editorial conundrums, keen insights she has shared with me for more than four decades.

NOTES

INTRODUCTION

1. The epigraph comes from the first edition. Elers Koch, *Forty Years a Forester* (Missoula MT: Mountain Press, 1998), 159.

2. Hamlin Garland, *Cavanagh, Forest Ranger: A Romance of the Mountain West* (New York: Harper & Brothers Publishers, 1910).

3. Ivan Doig, *English Creek* (New York: Atheneum, 1984); Elers Koch, *The High Trail* (Caldwell ID: The Caxton Printers, 1953).

4. Doig, *English Creek*, 98.

5. Garland, *Cavanagh*, 73.

6. Koch, *Forty Years a Forester*, 23.

7. Kim Allen Scott, ed., *Splendid on a Large Scale: The Writings of Hans Peter Koch, Montana Territory, 1869–1874* (Helena MT: Drumlummon Institute and Bedrock Editions, 2011); Koch, *Forty Years a Forester*, 24.

8. Koch, *Forty Years a Forester*, 33.

9. Char Miller, *Ground Work: Conservation in American Culture* (Durham NC: Forest History Society, 2007), 11–25; Shen Hou, *The City Natural: Garden and Forest Magazine and the Rise of American Environmentalism* (Pittsburgh PA: University of Pittsburgh Press, 2013).

10. "An Act Making Appropriations for Sundry Civil Expenses of the Government for the Fiscal Year Ending June Thirtieth, Eighteen Hundred and Ninety-Eight, and for other purposes," in *Annual Report of the Secretary of the Interior, 1897*, I: 114–17.

11. Char Miller, *Public Lands, Public Debates: A Century of Controversy* (Corvallis: Oregon State University Press, 2012), 16–31.

12. Bernhard E. Fernow, "The Providential Functions of Government with Special Reference to Natural Resources," *Science 2* (August 30, 1895): 252–54. For an analysis of Fernow's political philosophy, see Miller, *Ground Work*, 26–38.

13. Miller, *Ground Work*, 85–89; "greatest good" quote from Gifford Pinchot, *Breaking New Ground*, Commemorative Edition, (Washington DC: Island Press, 1998), 261.

14. Quotes from Kathryn L. McKay, *Trails of the Past: Historical Overview of the Flathead National Forest, Montana, 1800–1960* (Flathead National Forest, 1994), https://foresthistory.org/research-explore/us-forest-service-history/u-s-forest -service-publications/region-1-northern/trails-of-the-past/.

15. "Inaugural Address by President Charles Duniway," *Kaimin* (October 1908): 14.

16. Gifford Pinchot, "The Profession of Forestry," an address delivered before students of Yale University (Washington DC: The American Forestry Association, 1901), 6. One account of this particular talk at Yale reported that it "developed such an enthusiasm among the undergraduates, that many announced a desire to make [forestry] their life-work." *The Forester* 6, no. 4 (April 1900): 83. Koch was in good company.

17. Koch, *Forty Years a Forester*, 36.

18. Koch, *Forty Years a Forester*, 38.

19. Koch, *Forty Years a Forester*, 48.

20. Koch, *Forty Years a Forester*, 51; Theodore Roosevelt, Proclamation 596, Establishment of the Shasta Forest Reserve, October 3, 1905, http://www.presidency .ucsb.edu/ws/index.php?pid=69621. Anthony Godfrey, *The Ever-Changing View: A History of the National Forests in California* (Vallejo CA: USDA Forest Service, R5-FR-004, 2005), 73–74, indicates that the Shasta Reserve was established in September 1906; Roosevelt's establishing proclamation was actually a year earlier; by Proclamation 656, on September 24, 1906, President Roosevelt *enlarged* the Shasta Forest Reserve.

21. Theodore Catton, *American Indians and the Forest Service* (Tucson: University of Arizona Press, 2016), 9, 56, 254–55, 300–302; Mark David Spence, *Dispossessing the Wilderness: Indian Removal and the Making of the National Parks* (New York: Oxford University Press, 1999); Beth Rose Middleton, *Trust in the Land: New Directions in Tribal Conservation* (Tucson: University of Arizona Press, 2011); William Cronon, "The Trouble with Wilderness: Or, Getting Back to the Wrong Nature," in *Out of the Woods: Essays in Environmental History*, eds. Char Miller and Hal K. Rothman (Pittsburgh PA: University of Pittsburgh Press, 1997), 28–50.

22. Koch, *Forty Years a Forester*, 52–54; see also "The Passing of the Lolo Trail," this edition's last chapter.

23. Koch, *The High Trail*; Koch, *Forty Years a Forester*, 54, 52, 43.

24. Koch, *Forty Years a Forester*, 91.

25. Ben M. Huey, "Elers Koch: 40-Year Federal Forester," *Journal of Forestry* 47, no. 2 (February 1949): 113–14; other contributions include Elers Koch, "Reforestation in White Pine," *The Four L Bulletin* 6, no. 4 (1924): 10–12; Elers Koch, "The Future of Forest Lands in Montana and Idaho," *Journal of Forestry* 24, no. 5 (1926): 518–32; Elers Koch, "The Approaching Timber Shortage—Can It Be Avoided?" *Journal of Forestry* 28, no. 3 (1930): 295–301.

26. Koch, *Forty Years a Forester*, 165.

27. Henry S. Graves to M. H. Wolff, March 22, 1928, in "Letters and Telegrams Sent to Elers Koch to Commemorate the Twenty-Fifth Anniversary of His Services as a Professional Forester," Peter R. Koch Collection, Berkeley CA.

28. F. A. Silcox to Elers Koch, March 20, 1928 in "Letters and Telegrams Sent to Elers Koch to Commemorate the Twenty-Fifth Anniversary of His Services as a Professional Forester," Peter R. Koch Collection, Berkeley CA.

29. Raphael Zon to Elers Koch, March 19, 1928 in "Letters and Telegrams Sent to Elers Koch to Commemorate the Twenty-Fifth Anniversary of His Services as a Professional Forester," Peter R. Koch Collection, Berkeley CA.

30. James Glover, *A Wilderness Original: The Life of Bob Marshall* (Seattle WA: Mountaineers Books, 1986); Char Miller, "Change Agent: Bob Marshall," *Forest Magazine* (Winter 2005), http://mail.fseee.org/index.php?option=com_content&view=article&id=200055.

31. Robert Marshall, *The People's Forest* (New York: H. Smith and R. Hass, 1933). Elers Koch's copy of Marshall's book is in Peter R. Koch Collection, Berkeley CA.

32. J. N. Templer to Elers Koch, September 27, 1943, in "Letters and Telegrams Sent to Elers Koch to Commemorate the Twenty-Fifth Anniversary of His Services as a Professional Forester," Peter R. Koch Collection, Berkeley, CA.

33. Harry Gisborne to Elers Koch, October 4, 1943, in "Letters and Telegrams Sent to Elers Koch to Commemorate the Twenty-Fifth Anniversary of His Services as a Professional Forester," Peter R. Koch Collection, Berkeley, CA.

34. Elers Koch obituary, *The Missoulian*, November 22, 1954, The Selway-Bitterroot Wilderness History Project, University of Idaho Library Special Collections and Archives, http://digital.lib.uidaho.edu/cdm/ref/collection/sbw/id/236. The ascent of Granite Peak occurred in 1923, which situates this quote sometime in the 1930s.

35. Elers Koch, "Lewis & Clark Route Traced across the Bitterroots," *Oregon Historical Quarterly* 41, no. 2 (June 1940): 160–74; Elers Koch, "Big Game in Montana from Early Historical Records," *Journal of Wildlife Management* 5, no. 4 (October 1941): 357–70; Elers Koch, "Geographic Names of Western Montana, Northern Idaho," *Oregon Historical Quarterly* 49, no. 1 (March 1948): 50–62.

36. Elliott Coues, *History of the Expedition under the command of Lewis and Clark*, 4 vols. (New York: Francis P. Harper, 1893); Doig, *English Creek*; Norman Maclean, *Young Men and Fire* (Chicago: University of Chicago Press, 1972); Bernard DeVoto, *The Course of Empire* (Boston: Houghton Mifflin, 1962); Stephen J. Pyne, *Year of the Fires: The Story of the Great Fires of 1910* (New York: Viking Penguin, 2001). See also Hal K. Rothman, *"I'll Never Fight Fire With My Bare Hands Again": Recollections of the First Forest Rangers of the Inland Northwest* (Lawrence: University Press of Kansas, 1994); Timothy Egan, *The*

Big Burn: Teddy Roosevelt and the Fire That Saved America (Boston: Houghton Mifflin, 2009); and scores of other books.

37. C. M. Granger to Elers Koch, September 30, 1943, in "Letters and Telegrams Sent to Elers Koch to Commemorate the Twenty-Fifth Anniversary of His Services as a Professional Forester," Peter R. Koch Collection, Berkeley CA; Peter Koch, introduction to *Forty Years a Forester*, by Elers Koch (Missoula MT: Mountain Press Publishing Company, 1998), 7; Elers Koch obituary, *The Missoulian*, November 22, 1954.

38. Koch, *Forty Years a Forester*, 189.

39. Koch, *Forty Years a Forester*, 195.

40. See Elers Koch, "The Passing of the Lolo Trail," *Journal of Forestry* 33, no. 2 (February 1935): 98.

41. Franklin Reed, "The Facts for a Premise," *Journal of Forestry* 33, no. 2 (February 1935): 95–97; Earl W. Loveridge, "The Opposite Point of View," *Journal of Forestry* 33, no. 2 (February 1935): 105–10. See also Andrew J. Larson, "Introduction to the Article by Elers Koch: *The Passing of the Lolo Trail*," *Fire Ecology* 12, no. 1 (2016): 1–12. DOI:10.4996/fireecology.1201001.

42. Teresa Spezio, "Mountains in Every Direction: A Place-Based History of the Selway-Bitterroot Wilderness Area" (master's thesis, University of Oregon, 2000).

43. The Wilderness Act, Public Law 88-577 (16 U.S.C. 1131–1136), 88th Congress, Second Session, September 3, 1964, https://www.wilderness.net/NWPS /legisAct#2; Roderick Frazier Nash, *Wilderness and the American Mind*, 5th ed., (New Haven CT: Yale University Press, 2014) is the canonical analysis of how the concept of wilderness evolved in American culture and how the Wilderness Act itself came into being. See also Cronon, "The Trouble with Wilderness," 28–50.

I. MONTANA BOY

1. Kim Allen Scott, ed., *Splendid on a Large Scale: The Writings of Hans Peter Gyllembourg Koch, Montana Territory, 1869–1874* (Helena MT: Drumlummon Institute and Bedrock Editions, 2011).

2. Fort Benton, constructed in 1846 as the last fur-trading post on the upper Missouri River, is the centerpiece of the Fort Benton Historic District, a National Historic Site that the National Park Service has managed since its designation in 1961.

3. The county seat of Gallatin County, Bozeman was self-named by the town's founder, John M. Bozeman, in 1864.

4. Nelson Story, a gold miner, cattle rancher, and entrepreneur, was an early force in the establishment of Bozeman. He led a legendary 1886 cattle drive north from Texas to the Gallatin Valley and donated the initial acreage for what would

become Montana State University. Located in central Montana, the Judith Basin lies to the southeast of Great Falls and west of Lewistown; the Judith Mountains frame the basin's western edge.

5. Joseph Wright founded the newspaper in 1871, and although it would fold the next year, it reemerged as the *Courier* beginning in 1889 and continued into the twentieth century.

6. Lester S. Willson, a Union Army officer in the Civil War, arrived in Bozeman in 1867 and operated the eponymous store until 1915. Like Peter Koch, he also served on the first executive board of the Agricultural College of Montana.

7. Elers Koch was born December 12, 1880, in Bozeman, Montana; his brother Stanley was born there on June 3, 1882.

8. Richard Biering (1854–1929) married Thomasine "Sine" Koch, sister of Peter Koch's wife, Laurentze.

9. The horse's name was N—— Baby, an uncomfortable reminder of the casual racism embedded in American culture. Although it appeared four times in the first edition, in consultation with the Koch family and editorial staff at the University of Nebraska Press, I have elided the name in this edition.

10. Now Montana State University, the land-grant institution was founded in 1893 as the Agricultural College of the State of Montana. Peter Koch was an active member of its Board of Trustees, championing a liberal arts curriculum. Kim Allen Scott, who edited *Splendid on a Large Scale*, assessed Koch's comparative impact on the town and college: "Bozeman left his name, Story left a legend, but Koch left a university."

11. Professor E. V. Wilcox was a professor of biology and veterinary science.

12. Professor Frank W. Traphagen was professor of physics, chemistry, and geology.

13. Karl Jacoby, *Crimes Against Nature: Squatters, Poachers, Thieves, and the Hidden History of American Conservation* (Berkeley: University of California Press), 81–146, offers a close analysis of the U.S. Army's role in managing Yellowstone National Park.

14. The Gallatin River rises in the far northwestern corner of Yellowstone National Park, and near Three Forks, Montana, it merges with the Jefferson and Madison Rivers to form the Missouri River. Meriwether Lewis named the Gallatin after Albert Gallatin, the U.S. treasury secretary, and also named the other two rivers after the then-president and secretary of state.

15. William Wallace Wylie (1848–1930) came to Bozeman, Montana, from Iowa in 1878 as the principal of the city schools, later becoming Montana's state superintendent of schools. He made his first trip to Yellowstone National Park in 1880 and two years later published a guidebook to the park, *Yellowstone National Park, Or, the Great American Wonderland: A Complete Description of All the Wonders of the Park*, that laid the foundation for park tourism.

16. Elliot Coues (1842–1899), naturalist, ornithologist, U.S. Army surgeon, and historian, edited *The History of the Lewis and Clark Expedition*, 4 vols., (New York: Francis P. Harper, 1893).

17. Olin Dunbar Wheeler (1852–1925) worked for John Wesley Powell in the U.S. Geological Survey in the 1870s, and twenty years later he was responsible for producing the Northern Pacific Railroad's travel guide, *Wonderland*. In 1904 he published *The Trail of Lewis and Clark 1804–1904* in two heavily illustrated volumes. Hiram Martin Chittenden (1858–1917) was an engineer with the Army Corps of Engineers and a historian, writing books about the fur trade in the west, steamboat navigation, and Yellowstone National Park.

18. Ahern (1859–1940) and Pinchot (1865–1946) remained lifelong friends and collaborators, with Pinchot funding the publication of Ahern's *Deforested America* (Washington DC, 1928) and writing the foreword to it as well.

19. Cornell University also can claim to have offered the first full forestry curriculum in the United States. In the fall of 1898, Bernhard Fernow (1851–1923), as head of the U.S. Division of Forestry, launched the New York State College of Forestry on the Ithaca campus.

20. Pinchot replaced Bernhard Fernow as head of the USDA Division of Forestry on July 1, 1898.

21. Mount Rainier National Park was established on March 2, 1899, as the fifth national park in the United States; today it encompasses 236,381 acres.

22. The Yale Forest School, with a lead donation from the Pinchot family, opened its doors in 1900 and offered only graduate degrees in forestry; Dean Henry S. Graves (1871–1951) had known Pinchot while they were undergraduates at Yale; Miller, *Ground Work*, 77–86.

23. William Schlich, *A Manual of Forestry*, 3 vols. (London: Agnew and Bradbury, 1889–96).

24. Karl Gayer, *Der Waldbau* (Berlin: Verlagsbudhandlung Paul Parey, 1898).

25. William Howard Taft graduated from Yale in 1878.

2. GIFFORD PINCHOT'S YOUNG MEN

1. Dorr Skeels's legacy in regards to the Kootenai National Forest has been memorialized in a campground named for him. Containing seven campsites, it is adjacent to Bull Lake in a beautiful mountain setting approximately two miles from the Cabinet Mountains Wilderness Area's boundary in the Kootenai.

2. Olmsted was the son of the famed landscape architect, Frederick Law Olmsted, with whom Pinchot had worked on acquiring and managing the forests surrounding George W. Vanderbilt's Biltmore Estate in western North Carolina in the early 1890s.

3. Priest Lake is located in the northernmost portion of the Idaho Panhandle, and when Koch visited the site it was located within the Priest River Forest Reserve (established in 1897). In 1908, after Koch's inspection tour, the reserve was renamed Kaniksu National Forest, and in 1973 it was combined with the Coeur d'Alene and St. Joe National Forests to form the Idaho Panhandle National Forest.

4. The Crazies, as they are known locally, lie east of the continental divide and are located between the Musselshell and Yellowstone Rivers in Montana.

5. Gifford Pinchot recounts his first, test-filled encounter with Potter (1859–1944) in *Breaking New Ground* (Washington DC: Island Press, 1998), 177–82.

6. Now known as California foothill pine (*Pinus sabiniana*), it was dubbed "digger" as a pejorative term for its association with the Paiute Indians who utilized the tree's nuts for food.

7. The McCloud River drains an 800-square-mile portion of the Cascades Range, particularly Mount Shasta, and is a tributary of the Sacramento River.

8. Squaw Creek is also part of the larger Sacramento River watershed and is one of the tributaries to Shasta Lake that is not dammed.

9. This term, which gained legal sanction in the Chinese Exclusion Acts, was routinely used by whites across the United States to insist that Chinese immigrants were ineradicably foreign. See Frank H. Wu, *Yellow: Race in America Beyond Black and White* (New York: Basic Books, 2003).

10. Or sugan: a coarse blanket.

11. President Theodore Roosevelt designated the Shasta Forest Reserve on October 3, 1905, and then enlarged it the following September.

12. Founded in 1918, the Save the Redwoods League was as outgrowth of the Boone and Crockett Club and led by its members Madison Grant, John C. Merriam, and Henry Fairfield Osborn. Other club members, Stephen Mather and William Kent, donated the money for the initial land purchases. Susan R. Schrepfer, *The Fight to Save the Redwoods: A History of Environmental Reform, 1917–1978* (Madison: University of Wisconsin Press, 2001).

13. This is a reference to the massive and destructive mining operations in Butte, Montana.

14. The Malibu Ranch was owned by Frederick Hastings Rindge and May Knight Rindge, the fourth and last owners of the entire Rancho Malibu, and when Koch was there the Rindges were expanding the 13,330-acre tract to an estimated 17,000 acres.

15. Overton Price (1838–1907), English born and German trained, had worked for Pinchot at Biltmore Estate, joined the Bureau of Forestry as a forestry agent in 1899, and two years later became assistant chief of the agency. Pinchot credited him with being the agency's administrative genius: "He had more to

do with the good organization and high efficiency of the Government forest work than ever I had." Pinchot, *Breaking New Ground*, 143.

16. Saddlebags.

17. Neihart, Montana, home to about eight hundred people when Koch conducted his tests there, was a mining town located on Galena Creek in the Little Belt Mountains.

18. Michael Langohr (1860–1935) was the first supervisor of the Gallatin National Forest.

19. The forest was established on February 22, 1897, as the Lewis and Clarke Forest Reserve under the management of the U.S. General Land Office. On June 9, 1903, the Flathead Forest Reserve was added, and on March 2, 1907, its name was changed to the Lewis and Clark National Forest.

20. The Chinese Wall, cliff and peak, is in the White Cloud Mountains in Idaho and rises to 11,238 feet.

21. Haines was supervisor of the northern division of the Lewis and Clark reserve from 1904 to 1910.

22. Albert "Death on the Trails" Reynolds started as a forest ranger as early as 1905, then when much of the Flathead Forest Reserve was absorbed into Glacier National Park, he worked for the park between 1911 and 1913; C. Buchholtz, "The Diary of Albert Death-on-the-Trail Reynolds, Glacier National Park, 1912–1913," *Montana: The Magazine of Western History* 35, no. 1 (Winter 1985): 48–59.

23. In 1901, Frank Liebig, who gained his forestry training in Germany, became the first ranger assigned to the Flathead Forest Reserve and held various positions in the region until he retired in 1935; see https://foresthistory.org/research-explore /us-forest-service-history/u-s-forest-service-publications/region-1-northern /the-flathead-story/table-of-contents/chapters/frank-liebig/.

24. Fred Herrig met Roosevelt in North Dakota and fought with the future president as a Rough Rider. Roosevelt appointed him to his ranger's post in 1904. See "Fred Herrig Story," https://foresthistory.org/research-explore/us-forest -service-history/u-s-forest-service-publications/region-1-northern/the-flathead -story/table-of-contents/chapters/fred-herrig-story/.

25. Highwood Mountains National Forest was established as the Highwood Mountains Forest on April 12, 1906, with 45,080 acres. On July 1, 1908, the entire forest was combined with Little Belt, Snowy Mountains, and Little Rockies National Forests to create the Jefferson National Forest in Montana, which eventually would be folded into the Lewis and Clark National Forest.

26. Hired in 1904, James Thain was the first supervisor of the Highwood Mountains Forest Reserve, which Theodore Roosevelt established December 12, 1903, via Proclamation 511: http://www.presidency.ucsb.edu/ws/index.php?pid=69455.

27. Pinchot, *Breaking New Ground*, Commemorative Edition, 150–51, describes the founding principles of the SAF and its socializing purposes.

28. George Woodruff (1864–1934), another of Pinchot's Yale College classmates, was chief law officer for the U.S. Forest Service and later attorney general for the state of Pennsylvania, working, once again, for Governor Pinchot.

29. Theodore Roosevelt established the Madison Forest Reserve on August 16, 1902, and it comprised 736,000 acres. Its name was discontinued in December 1931 when its lands were redistributed between the Beaverhead, Gallatin, and Deerlodge National Forests.

30. Jasper Seely (1857–1907)—not *Seeley* as Koch spells his name—joined the Interior Department in 1898 to supervise its forested lands in Montana and transferred to the new Forest Service in 1905. Clearwater Lake, on which he and his family lived for many years, was renamed in the Seely family's honor (with its correct spelling).

31. Gerda Heiberg-Jürgensen was born in Denmark in 1880, daughter of Rasmus Emil Jürgensen and Ingeborg Marie Biering, and had once visited her Montana cousins—including a smitten Elers Koch; the two would marry in December 1906.

32. The Lolo National Forest was created in 1906 and currently contains two million acres; the Bitterroot, designated in 1898, encompasses 1.5 million acres; and the Missoula, founded in 1906, absorbed portions of the Hell Gate National Forest two years later and in December 1931 was divided between the Lolo and Deerlodge National Forests.

3. FOREST SUPERVISOR: 1907–1918

1. Three years after Hell Gate Forest Reserve was created in 1906 with 1.5 million acres, it was divided up between four western Montana national forests.

2. A. B. Hammond, who owned the eponymous building, was a controversial lumberman and entrepreneur whose career is deftly chronicled in Gregory Gordon, *When Money Grew on Trees: A. B. Hammond and the Age of the Timber Baron* (Norman: University of Oklahoma Press, 2014).

3. Wilford White later replaced Koch as supervisor of the Bitterroot National Forest, a position he held from 1909 to 1921.

4. Vardis Fisher (1898–1968) wrote a series of popular western novels.

5. Thomas R. Cox, *The Lumberman's Frontier: Three Centuries of Land Use, Society, and Change in America's Forests* (Corvallis: Oregon State University Press, 2010) probes the tradition that Koch describes.

6. In 1899 Wilkerson and another ranger, Henry C. Tuttle, built the cabin that Koch refers to, which today has been restored and is named the Alta Historic

Ranger Station, https://www.fs.usda.gov/detailfull/bitterroot/learning/history
-culture/?cid=STELPRDB5160446.

7. The St. Paul Tunnel was constructed as part of the Milwaukee Road's "Pacific
Coast Extension" project. Construction of the 8,771-foot-long tunnel began
in 1901 and was completed in 1909. The rail line was abandoned in 1980 and
has since been converted as a hiking and biking trail.

8. At the time, Haines was the acting supervisor of the Coeur d'Alene National
Forest.

9. Bright's disease is a historical term for a variety of kidney diseases.

10. William B. Greeley (1879–1955), who received his master's degree in forestry
at Yale in 1904, one year after Koch, served as regional forester from 1908 to
1911, became the assistant chief of silviculture, and later was the Forest Service's
third chief, from 1920 to 1928.

11. Graves did not follow his own advice, serving as a lt. colonel in one of the two
U.S. Army regiments of Forest Engineers; William Greeley also served in a
similar rank; https://foresthistory.org/digital-collections/world-war-10th-20th
-forestry-engineers/.

12. Established in 1907, the brainchild of McGarvey Cline of the Forest Service's
office of wood utilization, the Forest Products Lab has played a key role in
the evolution of the agency's scientific understanding of biofiber; https://
foresthistory.org/research-explore/us-forest-service-history/places/forest
-products-laboratory/.

13. The role the 10th and 20th Forestry Engineers played in World War I is detailed
here: https://foresthistory.org/digital-collections/world-war-10th-20th-forestry
-engineers/.

14. Earl H. Clapp (1877–1970) was made the head of the Forest Service research
branch in 1915, became associate chief in 1936, and three years later, with the
death of chief Ferdinand Silcox, was named acting chief of the agency until
1943.

15. The regional offices were located in Missoula.

4. FOREST FIRES

1. Stanley Koch, "Remember 1910!" *American Forests* 48, no. 7 (1942): 306–10;
see also Stephen J. Pyne, *Year of the Fires: The Story of the Great Fires of 1910*
(New York: Viking Penguin, 2001).

2. James N. Diehl (d. 1982) joined the Forest Service in 1924, worked on national
forests in Montana, Virginia, and Missouri, and was director of the agency's
division of cooperative fire control when he retired in 1963.

3. Harry Gisborne (1893–1949) was a legendary wildland fire scientist, working out
of the Rocky Mountain Research Station in Missoula. His death in 1949, while

field checking the site of the Mann Gulch Fire that killed thirteen firefighters, is referenced in Maclean's *Young Men and Fire*.

4. Ferdinand A. Silcox (1882–1939) would become the chief of the Forest Service in 1933 and serve until his death in 1939.

5. Erik Loomis, *Empire of Timber: Labor Unions and the Pacific Northwest Forests* (New York: Cambridge University Press, 2016) explores the labor activism that Koch refers to.

5. THE LOCHSA RIVER FIRE

1. The canyon, located in north-central Idaho, is in the Clearwater National Forest; Lewis and Clark trailed through the canyon in September 1805.

2. The Castle Butte Lookout in the Clearwater National Forest was first constructed in 1916, rebuilt in 1928, and in 2004 was listed on the National Historic Lookout Register.

6. THE MOOSE CREEK STORY

1. Major Frank Fenn (1853–1927) served in Idaho's territorial legislature, volunteered to fight in the Spanish-American War, and in 1901 became a supervisor of the Kooskia Forest Reserve.

7. SNOWSHOES

1. Robert Y. Stuart received his master's in forestry from the Yale Forest School three years after Koch, worked for the agency, served in France during World War I, headed Pennsylvania's forest agency under Governor Gifford Pinchot, and became the fourth chief of the Forest Service (from 1928 to 1933) following William B. Greeley's resignation. He died in 1933 after falling out of his office window.

2. Although "squaw wood" is slang for lower dead branches on conifers and pines that are perfect for fire-making, the term derives from Euro-Americans observing Native American women gathering kindling. Even as the settler colonists benefitted from this indigenous expertise, by appending "squaw" to wood, they doubly derogated those they learned from—as Indians and women.

3. In 1910 President Taft fired Gifford Pinchot for insubordination after the chief forester publicly criticized the administration's sale of coal leases in the Chugach National Forest, an action that generated considerable controversy, which ultimately led to Theodore Roosevelt entering the 1912 presidential election as the candidate of the Progressive Party and Woodrow Wilson winning the White House. Char Miller, *Gifford Pinchot and the Making of Modern Environmentalism* (Washington DC: Island Press, 2001), 208–26; 217–18.

4. Known now as Stuart Mountain or Stuart Peak, the 7,400-foot mountain is in the Rattlesnake Wilderness Area just north of Missoula.

8. MOUNTAIN CLIMBING

1. Edward Whymper, *Scrambles amongst the Alps in the Years 1860–69* (London: John Murray, 1871). Mentioned in the text is the title of the first edition of Whymper's book, which bears the slightly altered title *Scrambles in the Alps.*
2. A mining engineer, Kimball (1836–1913) helped develop the coal fields near Red Lodge, Montana, in 1902.
3. An intrepid mountaineer, Fred Inabnit never reached the summit of Granite Peak but had explored much of the Beartooth Mountains and handcrafted what is known as the Inabnit Map, showing the topography of the Beartooth, Absaroka, and Teton mountain ranges; it is displayed at the Museum of the Beartooths in Columbus, Montana.

9. GROWING TREES

1. Koch had the idea for the nursery in 1907, but after the 1910 fires the need for it magnified; by 1915, the nursery's stock of young trees amounted to ten million.
2. David Worth Clark (1902–1955) was a Democratic congressman and senator from Idaho and was the state's first native-born senator.
3. Koch is actually referring to Compton White Sr., a Democratic congressman from Idaho, who served in the U.S. House of Representatives from 1932 to 1946; he returned for one more term in 1948. His son did not enter Congress until 1962.
4. Established in 1911, in the immediate aftermath of the 1910 fires, the experiment station is located near the town of Priest River, Idaho.
5. Burton Kendall Wheeler (1882–1975) represented Montana in the U.S. Senate from 1923 until 1947.
6. James "Tama Jim" Wilson (1835–1920) served as Secretary of the Department of Agriculture from 1897 to 1913 under three different presidents.
7. James Rudolph Garfield (1865–1950), the son of President James A. Garfield, was the commissioner of corporations and secretary of the interior during Theodore Roosevelt's administration and a great friend of Gifford Pinchot.
8. Henry A. Wallace (1888–1965) was secretary of agriculture under Franklin Roosevelt from 1933 to 1940.
9. Rexford Guy Tugwell (1891–1979) was an economist, a member of FDR's brain trust, and the first head of the Resettlement Agency.
10. James A. Farley (1888–1976), a political powerhouse in New York politics, served as postmaster general under President Franklin Roosevelt and from that position managed the administration's patronage appointments.

10. RANGER STORIES

1. Frank Liebig, who received his forestry training in Germany, was ranger on the Flathead Forest Reserve in 1901, managing one million acres that today are part of Glacier National Park.
2. Sperry Glacier is on the north slope of Gunsight Mountain in Glacier National Park.
3. Avalanche Lake, located in Glacier National Park, receives meltwater flowing off Sperry Glacier.

11. THE FOREST SERVICE AND THE NEW DEAL

1. The Emergency Relief Administration, later named the Federal Emergency Relief Administration, was established in 1933 and funneled more than three billion dollars to states and localities to create an estimated twenty million new, unskilled jobs.
2. For a close evaluation of the CCC, see Neil M. Maher, *Nature's New Deal: The Civilian Conservation Corps and the Roots of the American Environmental Movement* (New York: Oxford University Press, 2009).
3. Koch's description of the African American CCC enrollees is unlike his discussion in this same paragraph about Jews and Italians. With the latter, he is quick to point out that he is not basing his conclusion on who they are but on their work experience. He offers no similar qualification for the black men he observes. Indeed, his prejudice is underscored by his references to these individuals as coming from Harlem and Africa and is consistent with the racial hostility African American CCC members endured in Idaho and Montana. See Olen Cole Jr., *The African American Experience in the Civilian Conservation Corps* (Gainesville: University Press of Florida, 1999), 4. Koch's bias is part of a larger pattern of discrimination against non-white men in the CCC. "Unable to become whiter by working in nature," Neil Maher observes, "African-American enrollees, like white and black women, remained outside the New Deal body politic." Maher, *Nature's New Deal*, 110.
4. The Works Progress Administration, later Works Projects Administration, underwrote billions of dollars' worth of public works projects, including roads, bridges, tunnels, airports, and other vital infrastructure. Note that Koch's critique of WPA projects in a subsequent paragraph does not account for the WPA's profound impact in urban areas.

INDEX

Page numbers in italics refer to illustrations.

Index

Index

Index

Index

Index

Index

Index

Index

Milton Keynes UK
Ingram Content Group UK Ltd.
UKHW011848020524
442038UK00018B/229

9 781496 213358